Designing the Future

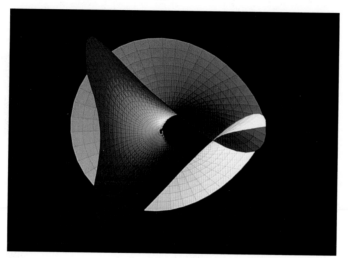

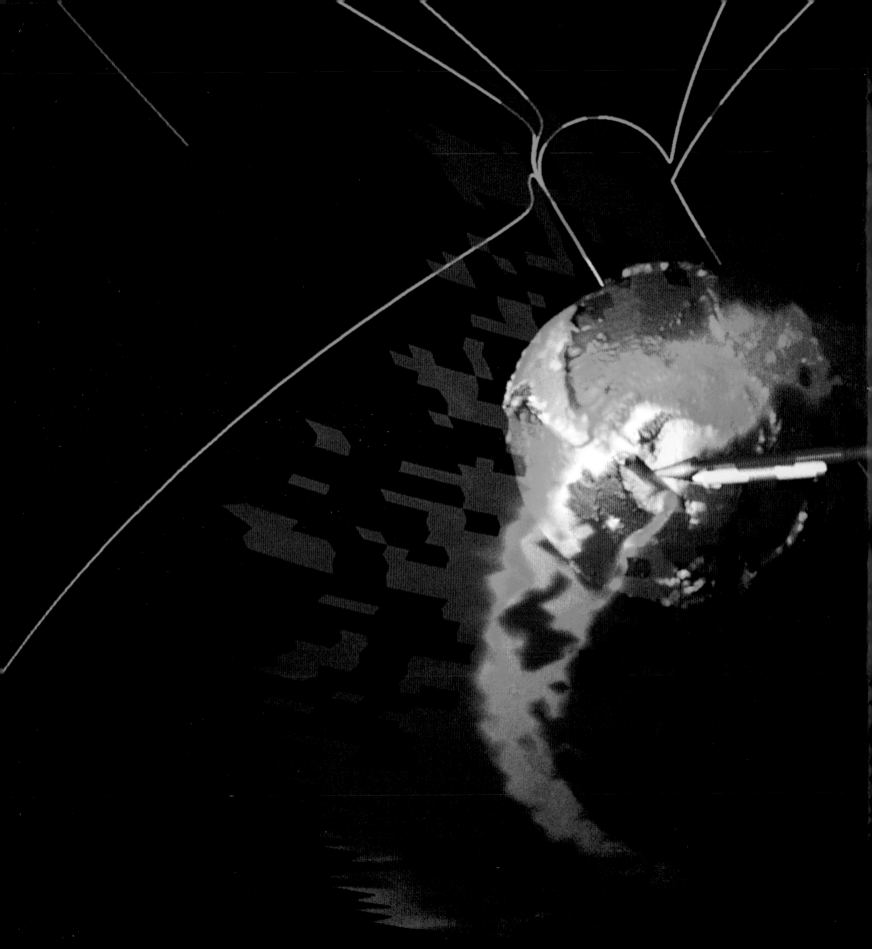

DESIGNING THE FUTURE

The Computer in Architecture and Design

ROBIN BAKER

THAMES AND HUDSON

To Kate, my wife – who bravely read many drafts

© 1993 Robin Baker
First published in the United States of America in 1993 by
Thames and Hudson Inc., 500 Fifth Avenue, New York, New York 10110

Library of Congress Catalog Card Number 93-60202

ISBN 0-500-01578-3

Printed and bound in Hong Kong

Contents

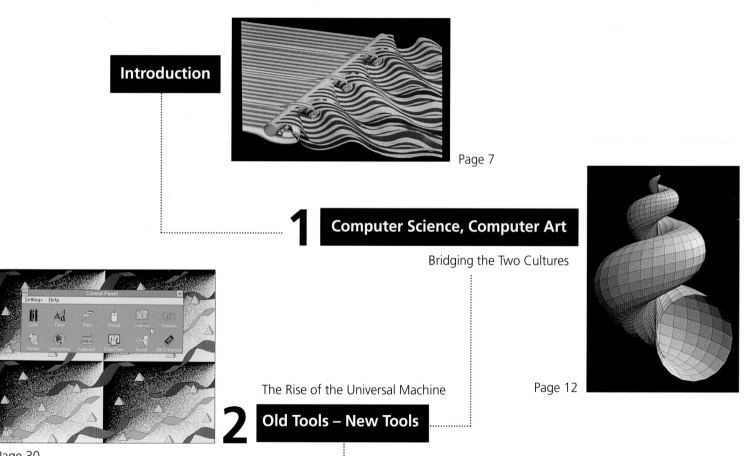

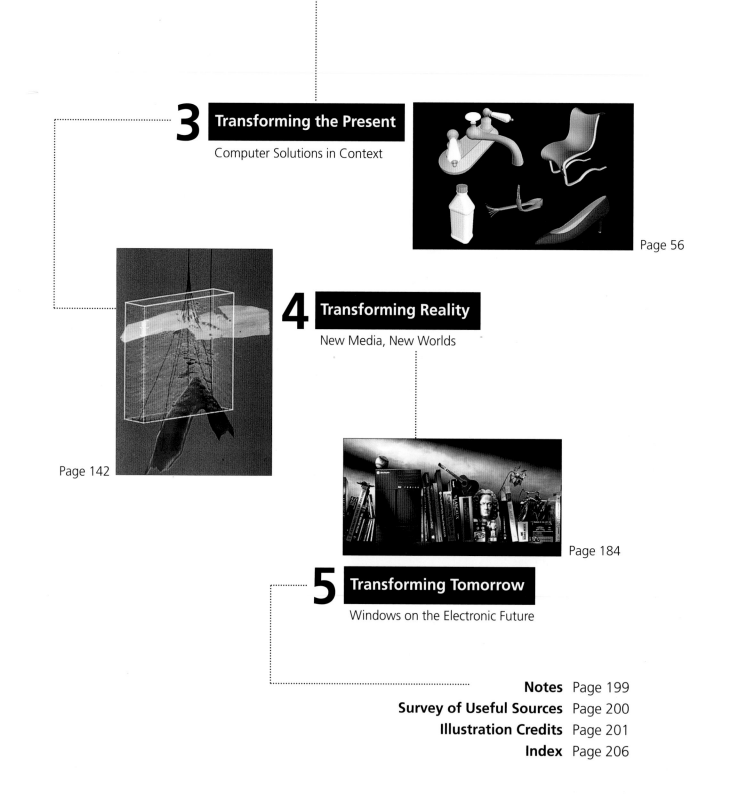

Introduction

The computer is a fact of everyday life. At this point in the late twentieth century we are witness to the myriad ways in which our lives are being altered by this machine, as it invades our homes and work. The human responses to this intrusion have been at opposite extremes. Some have seen the computer as a dehumanizing threat, ready to supplant human skills and knowledge in every area on which it encroaches. Others have seen it as a liberator, freeing people from drudgery and allowing them to concentrate on the more creative aspects of their work.

This is not a new dichotomy – variations on the debate have been endemic ever since technology first made inroads into our culture and society. Nevertheless, the development of the computer has forced us to consider afresh what we think about technology, to recognize that we cannot keep it in a separate compartment, divorced from the rest of our lives. The attempt to restrict technology to mundane tasks unconnected with our imaginative existence, to reinforce the separation of the technological and the creative, no longer works in the era of the computer. If we try to draw a boundary around our creative endeavour and to say that it has nothing to do with technology, the only result is that we are forced to redraw the boundary again and again.

In looking at creativity, Margaret Boden,[1] professor of psychology and philosophy at the University of Sussex, suggests an interpretation that she terms 'romantic', claiming that 'creativity – while not actually divine – is at least exceptional. Creative artists (and scientists) are said to be people gifted with a specific talent that others lack: insight or intuition. As for how intuitive insight actually functions, romantics offer only the vaguest suggestions. They see creativity as fundamentally unanalysable, and are deeply unsympathetic to the notion that a scientific account of it might one day be achieved.'

In looking at the creative use of the computer in art and design, I am unable to detect any fundamental problem with its imaginative use. I find little evidence that the computer inhibits creativity, or implies a narrow or constricted way of working. Nor do I see it as a threat, except in the minds of those whose creativity is already suspect.

Certainly, the relationship between human creativity and the computer is an emotive one, which causes feelings to rise on both sides of the argument, but this is only to be expected. For, as Joseph Weizenbaum, professor of computer science at the Massachusetts Institute of Technology, suggests:[2]

Today, as the computer brings the once-separate worlds of art and science ever closer together, technology and creativity are merging in many different fields – with exciting consequences. Right, main image: computer simulation of a design for the Mappin Terraces, London Zoo. Inset, right: computer-animated film still from *The Lawnmower Man.* Below: textile design by Malcom Cox. From architecture and automobile design to the film and fashion industries, the computer has firmly established itself as an art and design tool with unquestionable creative potential.

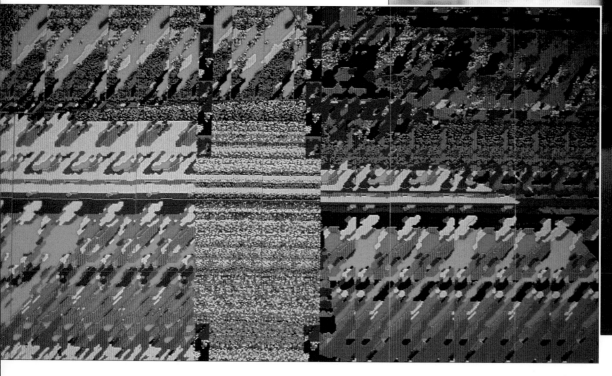

'One would expect man to cathect more intensely to instruments that couple directly to his own intellectual, cognitive, and emotive functions than to machines that merely extend the power of his muscles.'

Implicit throughout this book is the theme that the computer could be used as a bridge between the cultures of art and science. It could be used to chip away at the divisions that exist between the two, to the benefit of each. There are distinctions that can be drawn between these cultures, but we need to identify the similarities. The pages that follow are intended to help in that process.

When computing is referred to within the context of art and design, it may still be considered somewhat unusual, because it is not the 'usual' kind of computing. To many people, computing is something to do with itemized telephone bills or standard letters from utility companies that use data-processing techniques. They do not associate the computer with the making of images. For artists and designers, however, the making of images is central to their professional role.

Historically, there has always been a place for the visual element in computing, from the linking of the cathode ray tube to the computer in the mid-1950s, thus providing an image as a means of extracting information, to the recognition of computer graphics as a discipline in its own right. More recently, the Graphical User Interface (see p. 17), with its insistence on the visual icon, has become the predominant method of interacting with the computer for all users, not just those in the art and design community. The supremacy of the visual over the textual as a means of interaction has been recognized not only in the realm of the personal computer, but also in workstations and the interfaces to the increasingly redundant mainframe computer. Potentially, this could ensure an important role for the designer and visual artist.

A significant contribution has already been made to computer graphics by the visual artist employing traditional techniques of perspective representation. These techniques, familiar to the artist, have been used for centuries to create an illusion of depth. They were transcribed into the computer system and now form the basis of most three-dimensional modelling systems. But the relationship between the visually creative person and the computer does not just have a historical dimension. This book will examine many new disciplines, including multimedia, the human/computer interface and interaction design, process visualization and virtual reality. Without a contribution from the art and design community, these potentially exciting developments will become mere electronic techniques devoid of meaning and relevance. As the computer becomes a ubiquitous tool, the other skills that designers have – those of form-giving and of understanding the end-user's needs – are also very important.

Designers in many industries are becoming increasingly familiar with computer systems in the workplace. Traditional working practices are constantly having to be adapted to the new electronic environment. Below: a computer design and rendering system in action.

The computer can be seen as both tool and medium, depending on how it is used. By itself, it is simply electronic circuitry; but coupled with appropriate software it can mimic many traditional drawing and painting techniques, providing a host of innovative options that would not previously have been available.

The need to educate experts in the field of computing in art and design and to encourage greater awareness of the application of computing to all areas of study is now widely recognized. It is based on the assumption that institutions of higher education will need to be able to produce graduates who have the skills to keep pace with developments in technology, to apply them creatively to their work, and play a role in the technological future of their particular discipline. Throughout the world, universities and colleges have programmes of computing that, by and large, began in the mathematics or science courses and slowly moved across the curriculum until they reached art and design. Art and design students are, by their nature, inquisitive and unconventional beings, whose attitude to, and use of, computing reflects these predispositions, resulting in a 'soft' and largely qualitative approach.

It is now possible for artists and designers to begin to assess what the last two decades have meant in terms of the application of computing to their disciplines. Large numbers of students have graduated with increasing experience in the use of computer tools through their education, allowing them to become critically aware of the role of computing. Debates on its use and role abound and should be welcomed in a field where there is so much potential for the development of new hybrid techniques. Such debates should not be prescriptive, but should attempt to keep alive the possibility of different answers emerging, while both the education and practice of design deal with the issues raised by the new technologies. Many forms of computing are already essential to designers in their work: electronic page layout, animation software, three-dimensional modelling and rendering programs. It is therefore necessary for everyone to understand what will happen as computing begins to alter the internal structure of organizations, for rigid demarcations between disciplines will begin to fade.

The traditional relationship between technology and art has often been instructive, fertile and productive, but the computer goes much further, by challenging many of the boundaries of art and the practice of design. This challenge is part of a broader pattern involving culture, society and technology, and above all brings to the fore the choice that confronts us: either we design our future, or we have it determined for us. This book will seek to show, in the many areas of our lives on which the computer impinges – from the construction of our buildings to the design of our clothing – the huge potential for human creativity that it unleashes.

Architects are just one group of design professionals who have applied the computer to many aspects of their work. It is particularly suited to providing fully rendered simulations of proposed designs, for presentation to clients. Below: computer visualization of a scheme for a hotel.

COMPUTER SCIENCE, COMPUTER ART

Even before C.P. Snow had described the gulf between the two cultures in his famous lecture of 1959,[1] contemporary practitioners in both the arts and sciences had little understanding of the diversity of influences that, in earlier times, had linked them into one culture. At least until the eighteenth century, it was impossible to separate the artistic content of a work of art from its technological structure, for they formed a harmonious and integrated whole. Since the Industrial Revolution, however, much of art has become somewhat removed from everyday culture and from the technological base of contemporary society. Ironically, it is one of the most amazing pieces of technology ever invented – the computer – that provides the most hopeful prospect of rebuilding the bridge between art and science.

The idea that a machine could be used to perform automatic calculations, providing faultless results, had long been the dream of inventors in Europe and the United States, but it was two Americans, Presper Eckert and John Mauchly, who were finally attributed – in 1946 – with the development of the first fully electronic computer containing no moving parts. Called ENIAC (Electronic Numerical Integrator and Computer), it was used to prepare endless tables of ballistic calculations for the US army and to perform other kinds of labour-intensive tasks, proving that large electronic systems could achieve accurate results.

There were many operational breakdowns at first. It was also extremely difficult to program the machine, since there were no manuals, only wiring diagrams. For ENIAC to work on each new problem, it had to be rewired by repositioning many of the connections manually. This could take days and involved minute checking to ensure that the correct connections were operational; the actual computation took only minutes. It was not until the computer was able to store a set of instructions prepared in advance – a program – that the real benefit could be realized.

It would be impossible to consider the development of the mainframe computer without reference to IBM, who saw an opportunity in 1951 to enter the fledgling computer industry. Thus began a domination that was to last well into the early 1990s. The IBM electronic computer became the model for succeeding generations of mainframe computers. It dictated much of the conceptual framework for how computers were designed and used, including the image they projected in the media.

The computer was originally designed to be a mathematical tool for manipulating abstract symbols, but it was not until the television monitor was added that the results of computations could be seen. This visual, rather than written, result gave birth to the electronic image, which was eventually claimed by the artistic community as a new form of artistic expression. The development was a radical one, since the CRT (cathode ray tube) had never before been associated with computing. The early designers of computers had used the familiar peripherals – the printer and plotter – to record the output. As with many developments in computing, it was scientists working at the Massachusetts Institute of Technology (MIT) who first made the breakthrough in showing how the television monitor could be hooked up to the computer, while data, displayed as a graph, could be photographed on to 35mm film. Ever since this development, the computer has been synonymous with some form of visual display.

Initially, the mainframe computer, for the artist, seemed very remote, and early developments did little to fire the visual imagination. The whole process seemed distanced from the practical and visually sophisticated world of the artist and designer, who were content to continue using traditional media. In addition, the cost of the computer, designed for use by experts, meant that access was only possible within the academic community, and then only for those with considerable programming experience. Computer scientists were unable to see any serious role for artists, unless they were prepared to take on the mantle of programming. And since the artist was unable to ascribe any aesthetic value to the visual output, the relationship was at best uneasy. In spite of these difficulties, there were some – mainly computer scientists – who saw potential in the use of the image for visualizing scientific processes. Even then, all the output was on paper – plotted or printed – and therefore imitated centuries of mark-making. While the coupling of the television monitor and the computer was a useful development, its visual potential had yet to be fully exploited.

Eventually, a graduate student from MIT, Ivan Sutherland, with his doctoral thesis 'Sketchpad – A Man Machine Graphical Communication System', developed and prototyped an interactive computer system that laid the foundations of modern computer graphics. The size and complexity of the computer systems of the early 1960s have since been forgotten; the Whirlwind computer used by Sutherland weighed about 250 tons, contained 12,500 vacuum tubes and was the size of a large house. It is difficult to

Early computer systems tended to be large and unwieldy, and to occupy specially built, air-conditioned rooms. This IBM system 360, model 65, was typical of the period. It required specialist operators, who encouraged the myth in the public mind that computers were far too complex and inaccessible to be of use in their daily lives.

imagine anything less interactive and more inert than this computer. Yet Sutherland's work clearly showed how man and machine could begin to communicate graphically, and demonstrated that the interface between the user and the machine was an important arena for development. 'Sketchpad' (later called the 'Robotic draftsman') revealed the potential for non-computer scientists to be able to use a computer for engineering or other professional tasks, presaging the whole development of CAD (computer-aided design). This was possible because Sutherland's work introduced not an isolated, single invention, but a totally new set of methodologies, which were both to inform and to constrain many later developments in computer graphics.

The model for computing up until this time was the large mainframe computer, often sited centrally in an organization. To this, users would come with their punched cards, and the machine would process information in batches, with the users returning some time later to collect the results. While this suited the corporate environment, an increasing number of small- and medium-sized companies, as well as many individuals, were denied access to a computer because of their great size and prohibitive price.

The Palo Alto Research Centre (PARC) in California, established by Xerox in 1971, was also aware of this problem, and in 1979 produced the Alto. This machine began the revolutionary upward spiral that resulted in the personal computer. The Alto provided the individual with a personally dedicated computer power source with sufficient memory to store application programs, at an affordable cost. The stranglehold that the corporate machines had had on the computer industry was broken, providing the impetus for many companies to start up on the West Coast of the United States, and forming the basis for the growth of Silicon Valley. As a consequence, the computer began to move away from restricted, highly specialist use, and to become a universal consumer product – with all that that implies.

This book is not intended to provide a detailed technological overview of the development of the computer, but seeks to identify key reference points that have contributed to visual computing in the 1990s. Nevertheless, it is important to understand the intellectual background that has to a large extent defined the theoretical basis of the machine now called a computer.

A few scientists did begin to recognize the computer's aesthetic potential. The seagull image (right) is the work of Kenneth Knowlton and Leon Harmon, who worked at the Bell Laboratories. It was created by scanning a photograph, breaking the image into very small elements. The average brightness of each element was then computed; these levels were given a value, and an icon designed to match the required brightness was assigned to each level. Icons

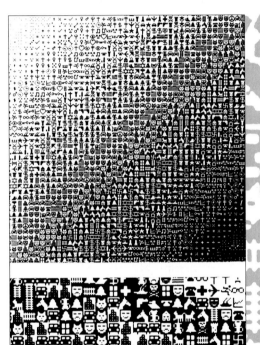

were also given the form of the main image – a bird, house, cat, face.

Left: many educational institutions used the computer to make drawings that represented a moving object by taking views from separate angles. This example, by Clive Richards (1970), shows six images, drawn by a mechanical plotter, from an animation entitled *Spinning Gazebo*. The software was severely limited, in that it could not perform 'hidden-line' removal.

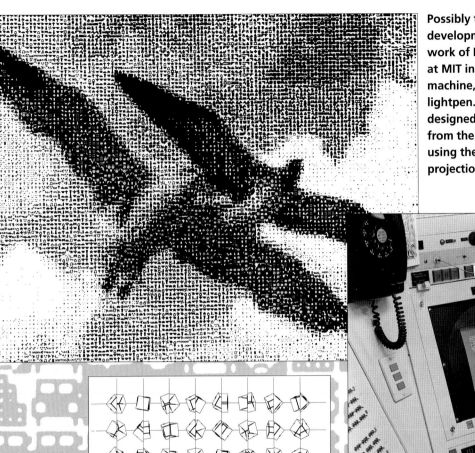

Possibly the most important turning point in the development of the visual use of computing was the work of Ivan Sutherland, shown below using 'Sketchpad' at MIT in 1962. He is using two hands to control the machine, one on the keyboard and the other holding the lightpen. This was always intended to be a practical system designed to look at real-world problems – as we can see from the chair image on the screen, which is displayed using the architectural convention of an orthogonal projection.

This 1977 drawing by Manfred Mohr is an example of a more sophisticated form of software, which provides variations on the theme of a rotated cube. The mathematical structure of the simple wireframe cube provides a visual complexity. Each image is divided into four quadrants; the positions of the top left and top right corners are static, but the positions of the other two are computed by a variable that includes several degrees of movement and rotation.

The work of Knowlton and Harmon underwent a popular degradation, as we can see from this popular Snoopy printout, which used computer code printed on a teletype machine. Most computer centres had variations on such images pinned to the walls.

Most classical machines have been designed to perform a single function; an aeroplane, for example, is designed to fly, a bicycle provides a very useful means of travelling over land – but both the aircraft and the bicycle would make a very bad boat. Since the Industrial Revolution, in particular, machines have been designed with a single purpose in mind; they have been conceived to fulfil a particular task and, if given other tasks, they usually fail miserably. In the mid-1930s, considerable thought was given to the philosophical and mathematical problems underlying this fact by an English mathematician, Alan Turing. Before then, many kinds of manual and automatic calculators had existed in Europe and the Far East that were able to perform addition, subtraction and multiplication, using data ranging from astrological tables to ocean tide tables. But it was not until Turing's work that the implication of such machines was realized.

Turing showed that it was theoretically possible to build a machine that would be able to perform a particular calculation, which transformed one set of numbers into another set of numbers by applying a few simple rules. The machine could then undertake another, entirely different problem by going through the same process of numerical transformation. Turing also saw that the rules that dictated the calculations could be built into a machine in the same way as the data that it was processing. So the idea of software (that included both data and application) was given a theoretical underpinning. More importantly, if the only function of the hardware was to obey the instructions in the software, hardware could take instructions from any software. Theoretically, one machine could then produce the work of any other machine and, in principle, could compute any task that was reducible to the appropriate code.

Because of this universal function, the theoretical machine became known as the Universal Machine, the Turing Machine, or – more correctly – the Universal Turing Machine. One of the main differences between the computer and all other machines follows from this: a computer has the ability (conceptually) to simulate all other machines. Taken a step further, this explains, in very general terms, why a computer can be a text processor or a spreadsheet, pay salary cheques, forecast the weather, run a railway and airline system, and so on. In the world of everyday things these are all very different and separate activities, but since they can be described in some basic procedural sense and translated into software, the computer has the ability to simulate them. The computer can therefore carry out all these activities and many more (depending on its programming), and, in this sense, is a universal machine.

So if the computer has this capacity, why should it not design or make art?

The experimental personal computer, called Alto (left), and the later Star interface were developed by Xerox to demonstrate techniques that are now familiar to computer designers. Most important was its emphasis on understanding the user's requirements. These were set out in a conceptual model developed before the computer was built – an approach that reversed the well-established tradition of designing the functionality of the system and hardware before considering the user's needs. Later, Apple were to modify the basis of the Xerox system in their screen design for the Lisa and then the Macintosh, thereby establishing the importance of the Graphical User Interface. It was not until the Macintosh II (above) series was produced that the Mac became firmly associated with visual computing, and was taken up by the art and design world.

Computers in the Realm of the Designer

Separating design from the many other kinds of creative human activity is difficult. It is a relatively new profession stemming, some would say, from the Industrial Revolution, with its central focus on the material culture of the manmade environment. From this standpoint there has gradually developed a body of knowledge represented by the view that there are 'things to know, ways of knowing them and finding out about them'[2] that are specific to design and distinct from more scholarly and scientific methods. The 'designerly way of knowing' has been identified in the attempt to understand how designers work. It is suggested that designers share a 'solution-focused strategy', which allows them to learn about a particular problem largely by generating a set of possible solutions to it. This is different from the more scientific definition of a solution as the result of a process of optimization or formal analysis.

Another expression of the 'designerly way of knowing' is the designer's ability both to 'read' and to 'write' in the material culture. By being able to understand what objects mean, the designer 'reads' the culture; by creating new objects that have novel messages, he or she is able to 'write' to it. This tends to happen via non-verbal codes that rely on graphic images in the form of the drawing, sketch, diagram and gesture: central aids to both the iterative development of an idea and its communication. Consequently, it is not surprising that the relationship between design and computing did not really have any substance until the development of the Graphical User Interface (GUI).

The introduction of the GUI and other methods of human/computer interaction did a great deal to change designers' perception of computing, since it allowed them, to an extent, to build on their previous experience. After all, designers were not seeking to use computers for their own sake; they just wanted to get on with the job. Early graphical interfaces assumed a model of the user that the designer could recognize. They encouraged a feeling of control over what was done, by allowing the user to display actions and anticipate results. The designer built up the confidence that the computer was consistent in action and reaction. The images used for icons were based on real-world objects, such as folders, files and dustbins, which the user could easily recognize and relate to their function. Human memory was not required to understand the task.

The use of icons helped designers to come to terms with the computer, but designers are, of course, just a sub-class of the more general user. What was interesting and helpful for the designer could also be applied to the lay user. The recognition of this fact enabled some of the more perceptive designers to take a role in designing the GUI itself. They were able to apply their visual skills to designing screen layouts, representing information and developing interaction scenarios, while also using their considerable formal repertoire to give shape and feel to the physical product. Nevertheless, the majority of designers continue to apply the new technology to their daily work without becoming actively involved in shaping it.

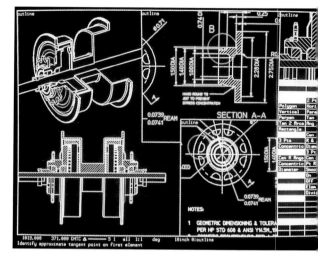

Designers have traditionally used the computer to amplify their professional skills, allowing them to carry out conventional tasks more quickly and more effectively. This is exemplified in the popularity of two-dimensional technical drawing systems, three-dimensional modelling and rendering software, and animation programs, all of which are common examples of the application of computers within today's design world.

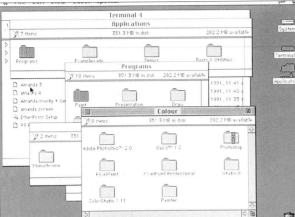

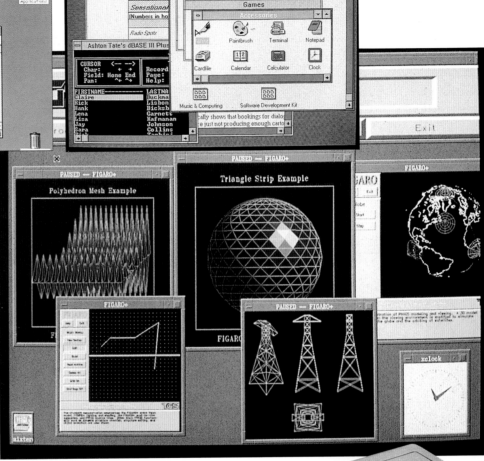

The Graphical User Interface of the Apple Macintosh computer (above left) was an early attempt to use a visual language to communicate instructions to the user. The interface is the 'place' where the computer and the user meet. In order to improve communication, Apple used the metaphor of the desktop, building on the user's direct experience of the office by using icons, or images, to represent folders, files and dustbins. The Macintosh interface was unique, and certainly the most mature expression of a developing visual language within computing that later formed the basis of many similar products. Other computer software producers began to recognize the value of this predominately visual environment and designed their interfaces accordingly. The Microsoft Corporation launched a software product, Windows (top right), mainly for the IBM personal computer and its clones. A software package called X Windows (centre right) was also developed for the expanding workstation market.

Of all the other ways of interacting with the computer, none has been as widely accepted as the mouse. Users took to this strange, single-handed device with real alacrity. The mouse was an integral part of the total WIMP (Windows, Icons, Mouse and Pointers) environment that characterized much of personal computing in the 1980s.

The late 1980s saw the development of many other physical devices that have begun to show how users can interact with the computer in more natural ways. The pen and digitizer were an early attempt to build on the user's ability to draw with conventional tools, and most computer paint systems used these

The helmet provides another form of interaction, which allows access to the new visual worlds. At first helmets were heavy and cumbersome, but recent models weigh only 1.6 kg and can be put on and taken off with ease. It is not only the peripherals

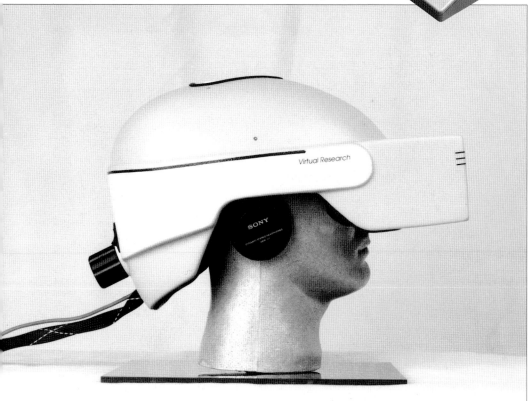

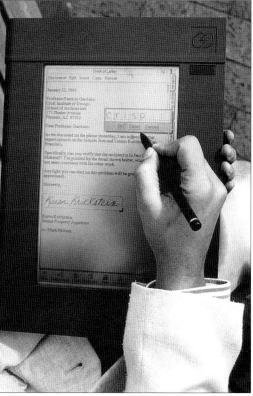

methods to control the software. More recently, the 'glove' – either an exoskeleton as shown above right, or a real glove – has proved an effective means of control. The glove has been used to drive complex machines, analyse human motion, steer robots, control animation and even music systems. Some models provide force-feedback, so that the user can 'feel' when an object has been grasped.

that have changed; computers have themselves undergone considerable transformations. They no longer have their traditional look and feel, with TV-like screens and keyboards. This is all part of the move towards more friendly, everyday computing. The electronic pen/notebook (right) will soon come into more general use. Lower cost, improved battery performance and more reliable handwriting recognition will by then make them indispensable items.

Computing is now essential to many designers through software packages that allow electronic page layout, typesetting, image manipulation and colour separation. Drafting and drawing software, as well as some three-dimensional modelling and rendering programs, are quickly moving from 'desirable' to 'required' in such fields as interior design, architecture and industrial design. Animation software allows designers to create moving images for presentation purposes, as well as providing two- and three-dimensional animation for film and television.

However, both designers and computer software engineers (who have always had a limited understanding of what constitutes visual design) have as yet been uncertain asbout exactly what kind of design is represented in the various application software packages. The 'designerly way of knowing' – or working – has often been interpreted as a series of stages (see p. 39). The design process starts with a briefing, and progresses through initial sketch ideas to a finished project and evaluation. But this analysis of the various stages involved tends to ignore the *classes* of design to which the process is applied.

It has been suggested[3] that there are three classes of design: routine, innovative and creative. Together these form a model for all design projects. In the first class of routine design the underlying assumption is that the design problem is well understood, and that the final design will only require that a prototypical model be refined, rather than radically altered. Innovative design is where the problem requires that various prototypical models be combined and modified to provide a new prototype. The third class, creative design, opens up the possibility of entirely new solutions, where even the design problem itself may well be novel.

If a survey were conducted into the uses of computing in both the teaching and practice of design, it would probably discover that very little has changed. What designers were doing before the introduction of computing they are still doing. The kinds of drawing and modelling employed are still conceptually the same, and the effect of computing on the nature of the final product has been marginal. The process by which products are conceived and represented has simply moved from traditional materials to electronic ones.

Computer-aided design (CAD) was first introduced into the design office to improve productivity. The well-worn arguments that underpinned this move were always concerned with the computer's ability to enhance current techniques, while ensuring that it did not interfere with solidly reliable, traditional work practices. From this it is simple to infer that most of the current software used by designers falls into the first class – that of routine design. This is because the conceptual framework of the software is dictated by the fact that production advantages can most readily be gained by modifying an existing solution.

The recent development of more 'open systems' of computing allows for an increasingly seamless movement of information from one computer system to another, or from one

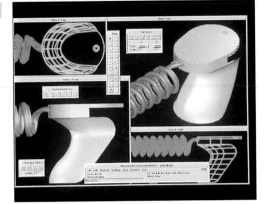

CAD (computer-aided design) systems like Microstation (above) and Pagemaker are now to be found in most design practices. They provide an electronic emulation of the traditional design office, offering page layout and enabling paint and image manipulation. Right: projected design for the chapel of Notre-Dame-de-Haut in Ronchamp – a three-dimensional modelling program used in the context of architecture.

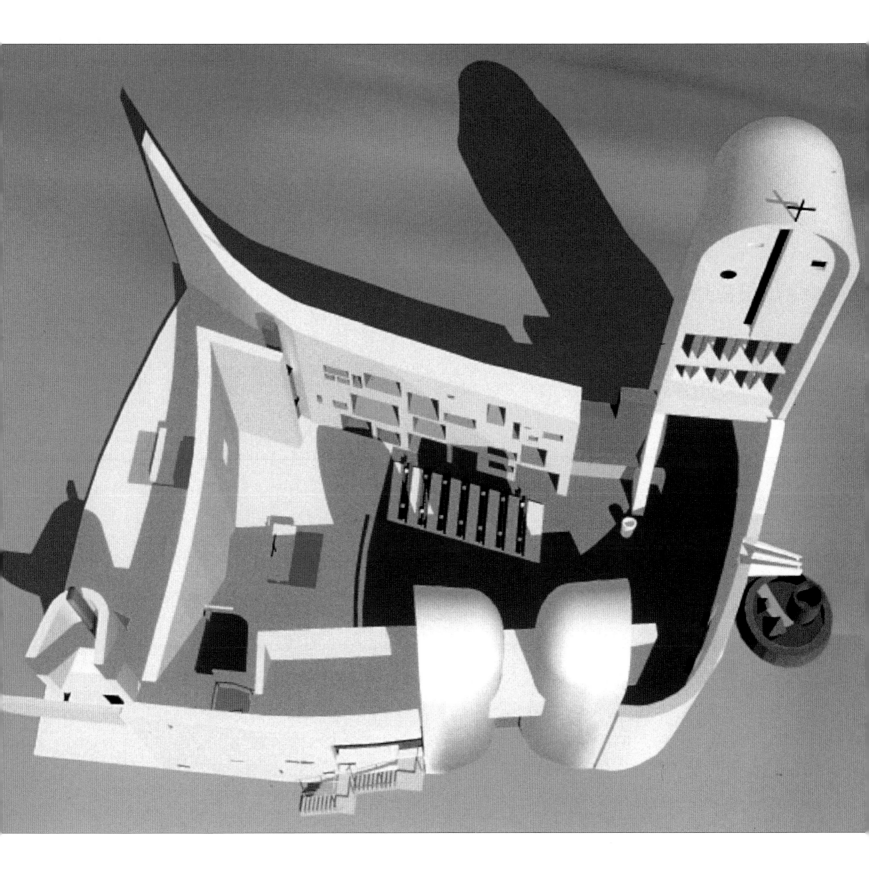

application to another. So much so, that the ability to combine solutions is now a practical and realizable possibility. This supports the second class of design: innovative design. However, it is difficult to find any software that supports the truly creative areas of design activity, particularly when most software systems lack the ability to contain imprecise or 'fuzzy' information, which is often the hallmark of creative design work, certainly in its early stages.

It is clear that to exploit fully the use of the computer in design, it will be necessary to change not only *what* is done but *how* it is done. This is the current dilemma that is causing so much concern in the design community, as it implies a fundamental restructuring of traditional processes.

Computer-generated Art

Although artists have become increasingly involved in producing computer-generated work, as we have seen they were initially put off by the lack of a visually mature language and the considerable programming expertise that was required. It was the work of the scientific community – with their early attempts to extract visual meaning from the computer – that provided the platform on which artists could build.

A catalyst in artistic development was an exhibition held in London at the ICA gallery in 1986. 'Cybernetic Serendipity – The Computer and the Arts', organized by Jasia Reichardt, brought together many of the creative practitioners in this new field. 'The aim is to present an area of activity which manifests artists' involvement with science, and the scientists' involvement with the arts.'[4] In the introduction to a special issue of *Studio International*, Reichardt comments on arguably the single most important revelation of this exhibition: 'The engineers, for whom the graphic plotter driven by a computer represented nothing more than a means of solving certain problems visually, have occasionally become so interested in the possibilities of this visual output, that they have started to make drawings which bear no practical application, and for which the only real motives are the desire to explore, and the sheer pleasure of seeing a drawing materialize. Thus people who would never have put pencil to paper, or brush to canvas, have started making images, both still and animated, which approximate and often look identical to what we call "art" and put in public galleries.'[5]

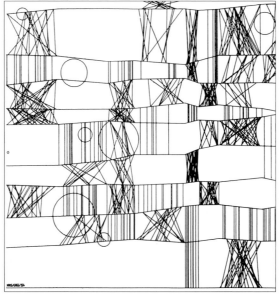

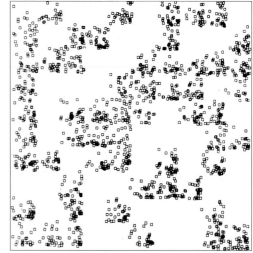

These two images by Frieder Nake, from the exhibition 'Cybernetic Serendipity', illustrate how mathematicians moved into the realm of the arts, establishing some of the parameters of the computer aesthetic. *Klee No.2* (left), first produced in 1965, is, significantly, named after an artist. The image below, *Computer Graphic*, was a prize-winning entry in what is believed to have been the first computer art competition, run by the magazine *Computers and Automation* in 1966.

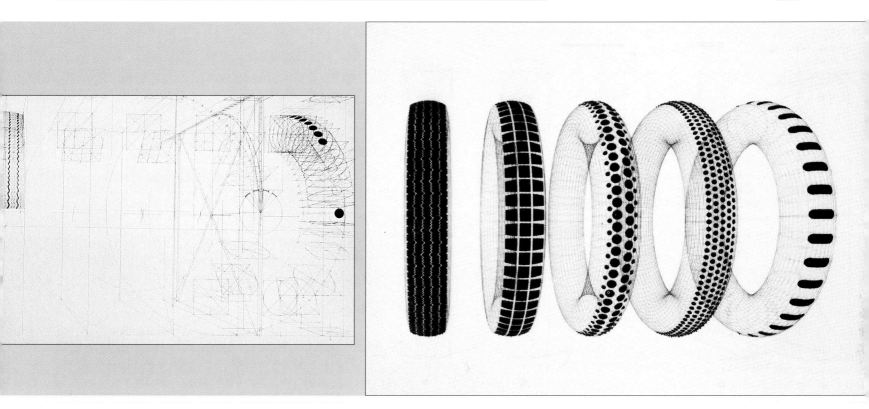

It is interesting that this extract concentrates on the scientific contribution to the arts, and does not mention the artist's role – although the exhibition did contain some notable examples by artists. Reichardt was later quoted as knowing only 'three artists who were producing computer graphics; all the other images were being made by scientists.'[6] This reinforces the view that most early attempts to inject computer-generated images with aesthetic meaning came from scientists rather than artists. The suggestion is supported by the earlier exhibition at the Howard Wise gallery in New York, in 1965, which had exhibited a digital graphics show of scientific work, including contributions by mathematician Michael Noll. In the same year Noll and two other mathematicians, Frieder Nake and George Nees, had held an exhibition in Stuttgart, Germany.

Artists took some time to follow the scientific lead in the development of the electronic image. It was not until the computer was widely affordable, or that artists were able to gain access via institutions that results began to appear. The artist was further hindered by the lack of appropriate software and of devices that could output in colour. There was also an intellectual climate of uncertainty about art produced by machine. By the 1980s many of these obstacles had been overcome, and because of the diversity of approach in the artistic realm, the restructuring that was necessary in the design field was not required. Computer systems provided an alternative approach that could be integrated with traditional media, or not, depending on the artist's preference.

Richard Hamilton came to the computer because it was too time-consuming to draw particular images by hand. For *Five Tyres Abandoned* (1964), shown left, he began by calculating each ellipse and then drawing it in perspective; but as this took so long, he eventually gave up the project. Some time later, in 1971, he discovered computer software that would do all the calculations for him, and so he completed the print now called *Five Tyres Remoulded*. His more recent work includes a series of paintings on Northern Ireland created with the Quantel Paintbox.

'Each artist possesses a weapon that allows him to intimidate tradition': Jeremy Gardiner uses this quotation from Fernand Léger to provide a key to his work. *Nature Morte* (1990), which takes the form of a large print, balances a number of separate images to create the still life. The work embraces both the laser-printed graphics of the Macintosh computer and the high-resolution photographic image-processing capability of the Quantel Paintbox. The combination of media makes for a lively interplay of textures, and offers creative possibilities that do not always exist in one medium alone. The project was proofed using dye sublimation technology, and the final print (right) is a lithograph.

Two major ways of making art with the computer seem to have emerged. The first, typified by 'paint systems', tends to emulate traditional techniques, although it adds others that are to be found only within the electronic paint system. Many artists, such as David Em and Joan Truckenbrod, have taken this route, while others, such as Karen Guzak, Jeremy Gardiner and Richard Hamilton, have combined electronically generated imagery with traditional painting techniques.

The second approach – algorithmic art – is a method of making images using rule-based techniques. It is exemplified by the work of Harold Cohen, an English artist now based in California, and by the fractals of Benoit Mandlebrot. It has been suggested[7] that if work produced on a computer paint system seeks primarily to represent appearance, then algorithmic work, such as that produced by Cohen, represents structure. This structure is knowledge – knowledge about the process of making art, rather than about the art object itself.

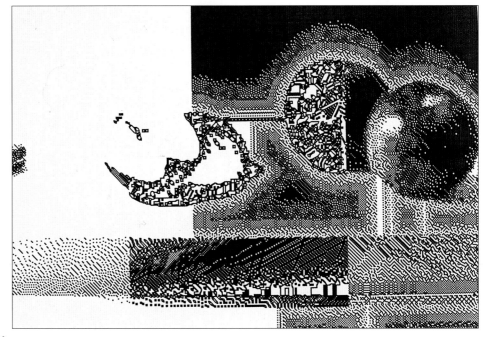

Knowledge-based computer programs can cover many fields and disciplines, but in Cohen's work the discipline is drawing. His 'Aaron' software consists of rules which are based on line-drawing and space-finding, for example. They are interpreted differently in each drawing, but do share a 'family resemblance'. This approach is covered more fully in Chapter Three (pp. 130–1).

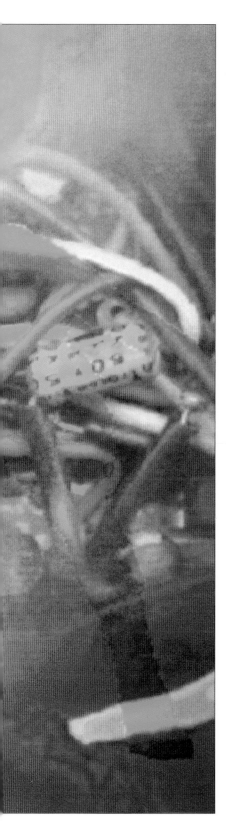

Far left: Joan Truckenbrod's images work on many different levels, from the pictorial to the abstract. She uses scanned images, photographs, paper cut-outs and drawings to create a sensation of layering and to examine the 'activated space' that surrounds people. In *Refraction Explosion,* as the figures interact, the auras that surround them merge to create the background colours. Various software packages allow the artist to work with many techniques, on both IBM and Macintosh machines, and to print out the resulting image on an ink-jet printer.

Jewels for Taj (above) is typical of Karen Guzak's lithographs. The initial imagery is worked out on the computer. Colour separations are then made, of about ten colours, and the image is finally printed as a lithograph. The crystal-like forms derive from drawings made by Guzak's father; he was a geologist, and it was from him that she inherited her interest in the creative tension between art and science.

Below: A typical fractal image which shows the 'self-similarity' principle in the linking together of the swirling forms.

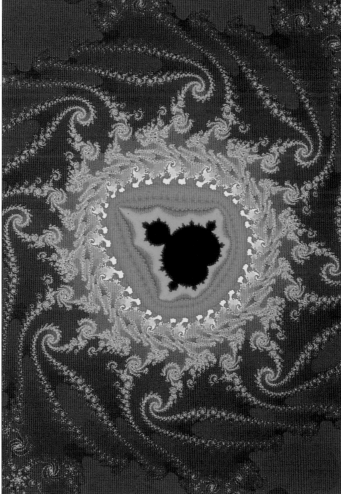

Fractals use a simple iterative calculation to produce shapes that appear self-similar at any scale. Images of mountain ranges and cloud formations have been created in this way. Programs to produce fractals appeared as early as 1985, with magazines providing code so that everyone could produce their own 'Mandelbrot set'. This media coverage was to some extent responsible for their popularity, but because they have become rather overexposed, much of the visual quality of fractals has been dissipated. Artists and designers seem to have taken relatively little interest in their development.

Most technologies require a period in which to mature, so that their unique qualities can be established. Computer technology is no exception. As Pamela McCorduck writes in her book on Harold Cohen, 'Typically, when somebody works with something for the first time, the really unique characteristics of the medium are what he [or she] exploits.... The computer offers things to the artist that simply don't exist in any other medium, things like the geometry or the tremendous detail ... or texture ... or light quality.'[8] It is probably too soon to comprehend exactly what all these unique characteristics are, but as technologies seem always to inherit aspects of their predecessors, concepts from traditional painting are bound to linger – in the same way that the idea of the horseless carriage was carried over into the conception and design of the motor car, that early cinema looked much like the theatre, until the full potential of the film camera was exploited, and that television was initially like 'watching' radio.

The work of 'computer artists' represents a transition from the traditional media of paint and canvas to that of the electronic world. It is interesting to note that most are happy to work in both areas, emphasizing the distinct advantage of exploring the crossover between the two.

Because of this dual approach, such artists are sensitized to the advantages and disadvantages of either field, and are therefore able to exploit them in some creative reciprocity. For example, when working with traditional painting techniques, decisions have to be made about how to proceed. The artist has to choose, and once the decision has been made and the image painted, that choice is confirmed; the other options are no longer available. With the computer, it is possible to 'save' the work, and then try out alternatives, to see where they lead, while still being able to return to the original starting point and experiment with other options. As the artist moves through each new creative space, further possibilities are opened up, and there is enormous potential to develop alternative approaches, because there is not much at stake. Providing care is taken to save copies at regular intervals, the artist can return to any point in the work. There is little resistance to exploring new possibilities, as the investment is minimal. Some see this as a major disadvantage with the technology, as it allows for a lack of commitment, while others see it as a positive advantage.

The idea of software emulating traditional media and providing an easy-to-use environment is still very controversial. Harold Cohen contests that 'The artist has never really needed his tools to be easy to use; that's a very common misunderstanding. He

needs them to be difficult to use – not impossible – but difficult. They have to be difficult enough to stimulate a sufficient level of creative performance, and you don't do that with something that's easy to use.'[9]

Nevertheless, most software paint packages are still designed to imitate traditional techniques, which means that users are encouraged to consider them purely as they would traditional media. Often, users seem comfortable with this, as they are not required to invent new methods, just copy old ones. The software developers are also happy with the situation: they know what to produce, copying traditional techniques as faithfully as possible; they do not have to invent new methods either.

An area of art exploration that lies outside both the traditional and algorithmic approaches is that of the computer installation. Jeoffrey Shaw is just one artist producing this kind of work. There are many who are designing and making structures and experiences that contain a significant computer-based element.

With the rise of a new generation of artists who are no longer intimidated by the computer, approaches to computer-generated art will inevitably diversify. And as we explore the full visual potential of the computer, perhaps we will be forced to redefine art as we know it.

The user of this interactive display, called *Legible City* (1989–90), can cycle through a virtual representation of either New York or Amsterdam. The image of the city, designed by Jeffrey Shaw, is projected onto a large video screen. The architecture of the street is replaced by the architecture of words, so that bicycling through the city becomes a journey of reading.

2 OLD TOOLS —NEW TOOLS

The relationship between humans and their tools is very complex. Using tools, we have been able to transform the physical world by developing cities, building bridges and constructing motorways. Through these endeavours, there has developed an awareness that the world is malleable, and from this awareness there has grown a visual culture of tremendous depth and texture. The tools have become ever more sophisticated – and the development of the computer provides perhaps the greatest opportunity yet to initiate overwhelming change.

Looking back over the history of artistic endeavour, we find several different tools capable of making a host of varied marks, from reed stylus to quill pen, and from paintbrush to airbrush. It is not the intention of this book to detail these tools, but to provide some general understanding about how they are used and how their use affects the marks that they make. The importance of these 'old' tools is incontrovertible, as they are the means by which Western visual culture has been created.

Drawing: from Creativity to Communication

Drawing is currently the central foundation upon which most traditional visual skills intimately depend. Artists and designers have long stressed the importance of drawing, considering it a basic skill without which the development of creative ideas would be exceptionally difficult. It is the tool that designers use to 'talk to themselves', as well as the means by which they externalize their ideas and communicate them to others.

Many authors suggest ways in which drawings can be categorized, according to the intention of the draughtsperson, in order to facilitate their critical assessment. In a recent book on *Drawing for Three-Dimensional Design*[1] drawings are seen as either a form of discipline, a means of externalizing thought, a medium of persuasion or a method of communication.

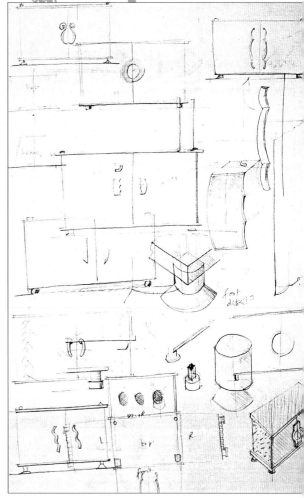

The use of drawing for training in observation and in the coordination of hand and eye has a long history, starting in fourteenth-century Italy. By the early eighteenth century, pedagogical drawing was an established fact in the art academies of Europe, and drawing classes continue to be offered in educational institutions up to the present day.

The second type of drawing allows the artist or designer to sort out ideas in a quick and responsive manner, so that the creative flow is not interrupted by such considerations as precision, cost or scale. This underlines the fact that drawing can be appreciated as a highly prized activity in its own right. The very act of developing an idea by making marks on paper seems to open the imagination, in turn encouraging the making of more marks.

When drawing is employed as a medium of persuasion, it is intended to convince a client that a particular idea would be the best solution to a problem. Most clients are unable to 'read' architectural plans or engineering drawings, so they rely on the visualization skills of designers to give them an accurate impression of the finished

The 'technical drawing' has been developed over a period of time to provide, as far as possible, unambiguous instructions for the manufacture or construction of an object. The conventions used in such drawings are understood by all professional parties. Generations of built-in skill have produced a complex, but very workable tool for communicating technical instructions.

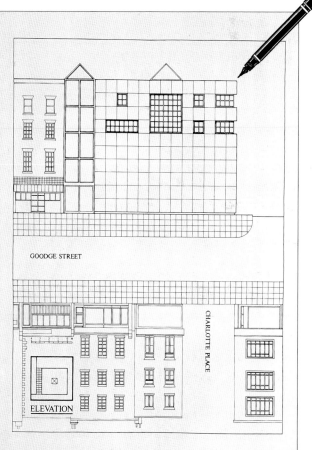

The designer's sketch (left) characterizes the stage when an idea is being developed. The drawing may not be clear to others, even to other designers, but it does communicate with the originator. It is loaded with many levels of intention – a potential that is represented by its unfinished state. Designers are particularly adept at visualizing how something will look, and producing a representation of it for the client's approval. Drawings like the one above have been the major means of communicating a designer's intentions to a lay audience.

GOODGE STREET

CHARLOTTE PLACE

ELEVATION

building or product. The architectural rendering, the interior perspective sketch and the artist's impression are all examples of this form of drawing.

And, lastly, a drawing is used as a method of communication when it is required to provide unambiguous information on how a design is to be made, built or manufactured. This represents, for designers, the point of separation between designer and maker. The use of the drawing as a utilitarian instrument characterized the rise of the nineteenth-century drawing office, with its emphasis on the division of labour. This was probably the most important manifestation of the modern separation between designing and making, between drawing and design. Drawing offices were set up with the single task of interpreting engineers' ideas and producing drawings for production. The bridges and ships of the nineteenth century required skilled and accurate engineering drawings, which were often sent to distant sites for manufacture. The drawing was often the only means of communication between the engineer, the manufacturer and the fabricator, all of whom understood the highly stylized conventions of the technical drawing.

Today, drawing still occupies a central position in art and design as an instrument for externalizing thought and giving form to the imagination. By implication, it may be used as a powerfully expressive medium, providing an unstructured, yet highly communicative environment. Drawing is such a flexible tool that it has been able to represent not only the sculptural ideas of Michelangelo and Henry Moore, but also engineering solutions by Isambard Kingdom Brunel and Joseph Paxton, and architectural plans from Andrea Palladio to Norman Foster and Robert Venturi. Italian product designers King & Miranda use drawing as the main way of representing their ideas, as do many fashion, ceramics, industrial and textile designers. The richness of expression achieved in these areas reveals the almost limitless ability of drawing to convey form and information within the many separate disciplines that make up our visual culture.

There are many reasons why drawing has established this central position in our culture, but some of the more pragmatic are often overlooked. In most circumstances, traditional drawing instruments and materials are very cheap; they come in many sizes and forms to suit the job in hand, and are often extremely portable. Pens, paper and pencils have been carried around by us for generations, certainly since adult literacy became commonplace and writing became widespread as a method of indirect communication. It is no accident that these 'tools' have formed the basis of both major expressions of culture: literature and the visual arts. Their ubiquitous presence has inhibited any rivals. Their integration into our lifestyle is now complete, and most people have learnt how to use them very effectively.

Below: an early illustration of the perspective drawing system developed by Leon Battista Alberti in the 1430s. He proposed a rational method for representing the three-dimensional world on a two-dimensional surface. This convention is just one of the tools that the visual artist has contributed to the representation of the visual world. This technique is so powerful and is so entrenched in our visual system that it was the obvious model for computer scientists to use.

As a pivot of visual culture, drawing has provided a unique solution to many of the practical problems of representation. With the Renaissance demand for increased realism in art, drawing was required to represent a three-dimensional world on a two-dimensional surface in a convincing and effective manner. Artists developed many techniques to achieve this, the most notable and universally accepted being the perspective drawing system. Many fourteenth-century Italian artists had begun to introduce perspective views into their works, but it was not until the early fifteenth

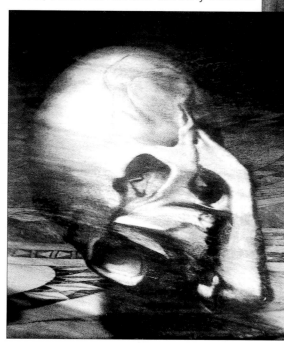

century that they achieved a systematic rendering of space that could be perceived as an accurate, illusionistic mirror of reality. It was the Italian humanist and architect Leon Battista Alberti who first described a rational system, in the 1430s, including the idea of a picture plane, a fixed viewing position and a central vanishing point. Since then, artists have developed perspective drawing systems with great success and conviction. The illusion of three-dimensional space on a two-dimensional surface is now an accepted part of our visual culture. Such was the power of the perspectival convention that there was no other model for the emergent technology of computing to follow, and it was natural that there should occur an ideological flow from one mechanical and mathematical system to another.

In *The Ambassadors* (1533) Hans Holbein uses perspective to manipulate the viewer. This early form of interaction between viewer and image, called anamorphosis, was designed to force the viewer to consider the painting from multiple positions. Initially the work appears to employ standard perspectival projections. However, in order to understand the odd diagonal smudge that appears in the lower part of the picture, it is necessary to view it from another position. Once this second perspective system comes into operation, the blur is revealed as a skull (detail, left).

The Transformation of Tools

For centuries, the absorption of tools into visual culture has continued at a slow but inevitable rate, reflecting the fusion that develops between the tool, the process of transformation it effects and the artisan who uses it. As Weizenbaum explains, 'In the act of designing implements to harrow the pliant soil, he [man] rehearses their action in his imagination. Moreover, since he is conscious of himself as a social creature and as one that will inevitably die, he is necessarily a teacher. His tools, whatever their primary practical function, are necessarily also pedagogical instruments.'[2] Thus, hand tools designed to shape wood or metal have clues to their use embedded in their very design. The positioning of the hands reflects the movement required and the amount of strength needed for the tool to perform its function correctly.

Pressure to modify the tool or work process occurs very slowly and over a considerable period, so changes are easily absorbed into the culture. A similar process of gradual transformation has occurred in the case of traditional art and design tools. Tools often require years of practice for their proper and efficient use, and artists and craftspeople devote many years to learning and practising skills. But as tools develop, more and more skill tends to be built into the tool itself, so the user needs less skill to use it. The mechanization of hand tools is an obvious example of this trend. The traditional tools of art and design therefore evolved through practical use, as their form was honed to fit their function. For example, the shape and structure of a paintbrush is now based on the type of paint used; an oilpainting brush is very different from a watercolour brush. A stencil brush has a very different handle shape from that of a paintbrush, with the length and thickness of the bristles essentially fitted to the very specific task of stencilling.

Tools that have been developed for the practice of art provide a very flexible working environment. The individual identity of the user is allowed to surface, because the tools impose very little restraint. As individual expression is not hampered or distorted by the tools, each artist can interpret their use differently, and direct them to produce specific visual characteristics – a personal style or 'handwriting' from which it is possible to determine authorship. This is why Gainsborough and Turner could use very similar tools but produce very different kinds of work, and why the brushstrokes of Goya are very different from those of Cézanne. The tools did not get in the way.

As tools are integrated into the culture of production, they take on a symbolic, as well as a utilitarian function. In the words of Weizenbaum: '... tools and machines do not merely signify man's imaginativeness and creative reach, and they are certainly not important merely as instruments for the transformation of a malleable earth: they are pregnant symbols in themselves. They symbolize the activities they enable.... An oar is a tool for rowing, and it represents the skill of rowing in its whole complexity. No one who has not rowed can see an oar as truly an oar ... a tool is a model for its own reproduction and a script for the enactment of the skill it symbolizes.[3]

The gradual, natural process of honing tools to fit the user's specific needs was largely destroyed in the nineteenth century by the Industrial Revolution, as considerations of mass manufacture and mechanization came to the fore. Recent moves towards 'user-centred' design, facilitated by the computer, may enable us to reintroduce something of the subtle, interactive relationship that once existed between user and tool.

Tools in the Changing World of Design

Not surprisingly, the use of traditional tools spilled over, through their symbiotic use in art and the crafts, into design and its related practices. What other models were there to follow than the pen, brush, paper and pencil? There is a confidence that derives from inheriting such tools. They have a proven record of success spanning centuries; they are trusted, because it is known from long experience how they react in use, and because they are so much a part of our understanding and appreciation of the past.

The rise of computing and its introduction into design is really the first significant challenge to these traditional tools. It challenges their continued use and appropriateness. This dilemma is causing considerable disquiet in the design community throughout the developed world. In judging the new technologies, designers compare their performance with that of the old tools. Their expectations are that they should be at least as good as the old tools. Otherwise, why change?

The nature of the design task is changing. What designers do and how they do it is undergoing a significant transformation, and it is likely that the old tools will not be able to cope with the new and accelerating demands. Three major reasons are often given to support the need to change from old tools to new tools: increasing problem complexity; the search for a competitive edge; and, most importantly, the development of new products. Although these are central issues that justify the transfer from old to new, it is important to remember that a whole host of further contributory factors also exists.

A good example of increasing problem complexity is provided by the transition that has taken place in the aerospace industries. The oldest companies in the United States and Western Europe have a history of building aircraft that dates back to the beginning of the twentieth century. The Second World War matured the production of the fighting aircraft, but at this stage planes were still drawn and built by hand with a considerable amount of craft skill. Once the war was over, and flying began to be in popular demand, there developed the need for more complex and sophisticated design to produce safe bulk transportation. This meant that new production methods were essential. Much of the early application of computers in design was initiated by aircraft companies such as McDonnell Douglas and Boeing. Today, it is inconceivable that an aircraft should be designed or manufactured without the use of computers. Such projects are far too complex and require such high safety-critical factors, that designing and building them by hand is simply not a serious proposition.

The same view could be taken of the motor car industry. While the car remained an enthusiast's toy, in the early part of the twentieth century, it could be designed and built by hand. But once it had become a consumer product, expectations of performance, safety and styling rose alongside demand. To meet these fast-changing needs, particularly in the area of styling, motor car manufacturers turned to computer-aided design systems.

Both the aircraft and automobile industries were in existence before the development of computers, and so it was a matter – not necessarily a small matter – of adjusting the product to meet the demands of the new technologies. Weizenbaum describes the process as follows: 'The computer becomes an indispensable component of any structure once it is so thoroughly integrated with the structure, so enmeshed in various substructures, that it can no longer be factored out without fatally impairing the whole structure.... It is true that, were all computers suddenly to disappear, much of the modern industrialized and militarized world would be thrown into great confusion and possibly utter chaos.'[4]

The second reason for moving from the old tools to the new ones is that modern technology provides a competitive edge that enables companies to perform better and to outpace their rivals. This argument is still very popular among computer vendors, and was a common way, in the 1980s, of justifying the vast costs necessary to equip a company with the new computer tools. There is now much more scepticism about this claim, as it is very difficult to obtain hard evidence to prove the point. Recent thinking certainly seems to indicate that the reverse is true – not to introduce the new technologies will be a distinct competitive disadvantage. However, much soft evidence has accrued to demonstrate that the advantage gained by the introduction of new technology depends largely on how that technology is managed.

Briefly, the argument for the competitive advantage to be gained by introducing computing, particularly in the area of design, is based on an increasing globalization of the marketplace. As companies seek to expand their market share, they tend to rely on economies derived from an increased scale of production, producing longer and longer runs of the same product. Conventional wisdom states that the more you produce, the cheaper your product becomes.

As the parameters of constructional techniques and material costs are highly specified, allowing little room for manoeuvre, products tend to be very similar, irrespective of the company producing them. Design is therefore vital to differentiate one company's product from that of another. And computing, particularly computer-aided design (CAD), can offer an increasing number of design alternatives. As the designer's responsibility increases, CAD has been added to the list of essential design skills, as Christopher Lorenz suggests: 'despite the introduction of product managers ... [the designer] is often the only person involved with a new product throughout the entire development and production process ... and provided the designer can become computer-literate, he or she has the opportunity to gain still greater influence.'[5]

The work of William Fetter has gone largely unnoticed in the computing world. The Boeing Aircraft Corporation, where he worked, has been an important innovator because of the size and complexity of its products. In its search for more economic design and production methods, it has used the computer in experimental situations. It was Boeing that first coined the term 'computer graphics' to describe the amalgamation of the traditional graphic design process and the new technology. Fetter developed the use of a manikin that represented the average pilot of the US airforce. These drawings were an early attempt to use the computer to simulate ergonomics; they provided data that was used in the design and layout of cockpits.

The automobile industry also became an early user of computer systems, in engineering, production and styling, as their products became more complex and consumer-driven. The need to cut development times was essential in a highly

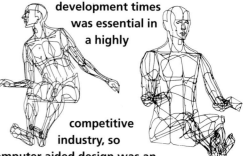

competitive industry, so computer-aided design was an important tool. Attempts have been made by large industrial organizations to develop their own computer products, rather than have an existing product tailored to their needs. The Computer Design and Rendering System (CDRS) was developed jointly by car manufacturers and the Evans & Sutherland computer company. Right: a computer-generated visualization of two cars in a showroom. The designer's expertise is evident in the realistic reflections.

The third area where old tools have become increasingly unproductive is in products that have been invented as a result of new technologies. On 12 April 1961 US radar detected a rocket launch from the Soviet launch station in Baikonur. The space race had begun. The political and military pressure in the US to place a man on the moon before the end of the decade provided the necessary impetus to produce faster, more efficient and powerful computers. These were to be a pivotal factor in the exploration of space. At the centre of this machine was the microchip.

If there is any product that is going to change the face of our lives and culture, then it is the microchip, the most influential development since the invention of printing. The chip has a set of characteristics unknown in any other product. It is among the most complex, the most powerful, the smallest, fastest and least expensive of products. It requires a degree of precision for its own production that could not be achieved without the use of computers. The chip reverses the classic balance of traditional industries, by

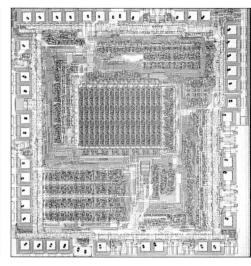

The microchip is the core of the computer. It is one of the most technologically sophisticated products to have come out of the twentieth century. As objects in their own right, microchips are often very beautiful; the complexity of the intricate tracery of connections can only be fully appreciated when they are enlarged. Unlike most nineteenth-, or even some twentieth-century machines, they give no visual clue to their operation or function; to all intents and purposes they could be decorative tapestries. This chip, from VLSI Technology Inc., is an example of a gate array. Made in 1986, it has a density of 33,500 transistors.

which the costs of manufacture far outweigh pre-production and planning costs. The most expensive part by far of the production of a chip is the planning of the circuits and the network of components. The production costs are minimal. The miniaturization of the microchip is advancing so rapidly that it could disappear as a visible object. And this raises an interesting question: how will we relate to a product that is going to affect our lives in so many ways if it becomes completely inaccessible to our senses?

The new products are not only physical – as in the case of consumer electronics – but exist on the new boundary between hardware and software. Even such elements as the human/computer interface are becoming legitimate areas of design activity, and as the old design disciplines wane, many new ones will emerge to take over the core business of design. This is addressed in Chapter Four (p. 142).

While the transition from the old tools to the new is inevitable, it is useful to look at this development critically – as most designers do – because it is important to ensure that what is happening is well understood. It is often the case that the new technology is still having problems supplying a solution that has already been very adequately answered by traditional methods.

In 1969 the US put the first man on the moon. The design of the rocket and space craft was an engineering problem that had never really been tackled before with such a single-minded sense of purpose. Everyone involved was intensely aware of the fact that there was no room for error. The planning and production, which included the mammoth calculations required to indicate the correct trajectory to place the spaceman on the moon, were performed relatively quickly. Without the computer, this task would have been almost impossible.

The US was able to send rockets some hundreds of thousands of miles with almost pinpoint accuracy, and then get the space module back to earth – a truly momentous task. But Donald Michie and Rory Johnson[6] say 'getting a robot to guide a spacecraft to

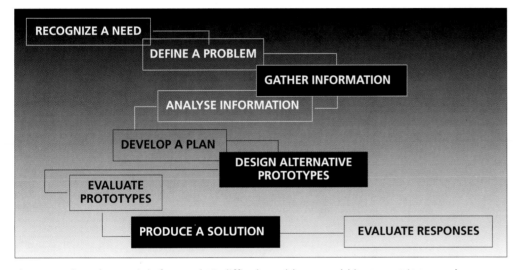

In an article entitled 'Media Myths and Computer Graphics', Patrick Whitney lists nine steps that form the design process and argues that currently we only apply computers to steps three, six and eight. The challenge, he feels, is to find ways of applying the computer to the other steps.

the moon is today straightforward. A difficult problem would be to get it to go down to the corner of the road and buy a package of cigarettes.' This demonstrates that computing, even today, is unable to deal with unforeseen events. If all the possible variations that can occur within a given problem are limited and can be written into the program, so that the computer model of the world is complete, then the machine can deal with the problem. However, most real situations, including design, are highly complex, and the possible variations are extensive. If the machine cannot learn from its own experience, then the accuracy of the program has to be of such a high order that it would be impossible to write.

Creativity in design is a very complex phenomenon – much more so than going to the corner shop for the cigarettes. As a consequence, it is important to apply computing to those areas of design where computers are useful and able to cope with the complexity that is required. This limit of applicability is not a stationary line, but a frontier that moves constantly as computers become more powerful and begin to understand more about the world around them.

Nevertheless, the kind of design that is involved in new technologies, such as microchip production, is very different from the visual design that is the focus of this book. The kinds of design that ordinary designers cope with, on a day-to-day basis, will increasingly be characterized by a computational approach rather than a handmade one. In this context, traditional tools will no longer be adequate.

So what is the designers' role in all this? Can they affect the way the technology is going to move? Can they bring designerly skills to bear on the problem of how technology is applied to visual design?

The New Tools

As we have seen, the domination of drawing and painting within the sphere of visual expression had a major impact on the evolution of the early computer tools; they were strongly influenced by traditional practices and tools. The development of computer graphics is still young, and in many cases when the software was written there were no models to follow beyond what already existed in the fields of art and design. The early phase of software development tended to borrow a set of past conventions and build them into the electronic environment.

A transition is becoming evident, however, in the new generation of computer tools that are being developed for use in art and design. While they are given the name of 'new' tools to distinguish them from the more traditional ones, they are more properly described as 'transitional', because they continue to lean heavily on their historic roots for both definition and purpose.

Weizenbaum writes: 'To say that the computer was initially used mainly to do things pretty much as they had always been done, except to do them more rapidly or, by some criteria, more efficiently, is not to distinguish it from other tools. Only rarely, if indeed ever, are a tool and an altogether original job it is to do, invented together. Tools as symbols, however, invite their imaginative displacement into other than their original contexts. In their new frames of reference, that is, as new symbols in an already established imaginative calculus, they may themselves be transformed, and may even transform the original prescriptive calculus. These transformations may, in turn, create entirely new problems that then engender the invention of hitherto literally unimaginable tools.'[7] The new software tools are in a transitional stage, inviting their 'imaginative displacement'. As yet, however, there are very few cases where this has been achieved; they are moving from the original context, seeking new frames of reference, while still holding on to their connection with the past.

With this in mind, artists and designers should focus on the computing tools that are increasingly being used in design and assess whether they do, or do not, make good substitutes for the tools they are replacing. More importantly, they must address the question of what these new tools have to offer during this stage of transformation.

Paint Systems

Credit for the development of the generic paint system goes to two Americans, Richard Shoup and Alvey Ray Smith. In 1975 they produced a hardware and software product

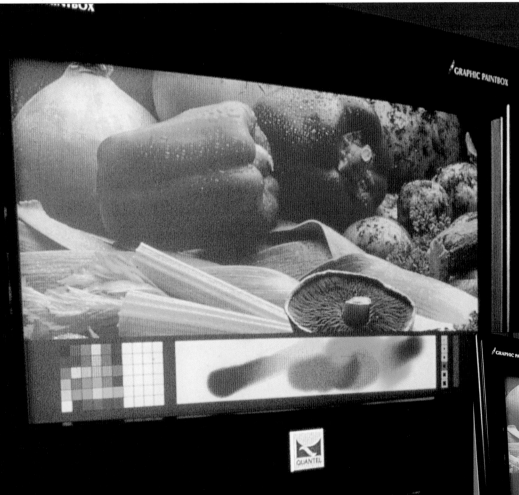

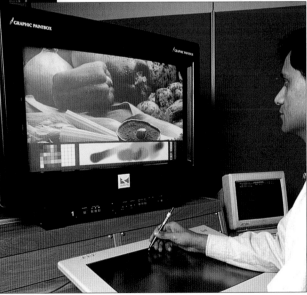

One of the most popular – if expensive – paint systems is the Quantel Paintbox, which has been used in many design disciplines. This was the machine used in a series of television programmes produced by the BBC, entitled *Painting with Light*. David Hockney, Howard Hodgkin, Larry Rivers and Sidney Nolan all used the paintbox to create images while being filmed, so that their comments on what was happening became part of the programme.

called 'Paint'. This was the prototype for the hundreds of other paint systems that have been written over the years.

Readers will probably be familiar with these systems, which allow the user to work within the framework of conventional painting, using electronic brushes and colour palettes. The popularity of this type of software is in part based on the integration of the traditional metaphor of painting.

An artistic use of the computer paint system is seen in the work of Stephen Pochin, who uses a layering technique to build up the density of his images. As electronic montage is ideally suited to the computer, this paper-based technique is considerably enhanced by the process.

Weekend Weather

Thursday	☀	75°
Friday	⚡	85°
Saturday	🌧	78°

Paint systems have been extensively used in broadcast television. A typical shot for a weather forecast shows a detailed background of the sky, against which appear the predictions for the weekend. The computer is ideal for such work, which has to be done quickly, under considerable commercial pressure and to communicate simple facts in a visually appealing way.

The user feels at ease with the new tools because they share some similarities with the way that artists and designers have always worked. For instance, a computer 'brush' can be selected from a range of sizes, each of which makes a mark of the appropriate size when in contact with the digitizer. Colours are selected from a 'palette', mixed to create the correct tone, and applied to the image as the user wishes. The results are displayed on the monitor almost simultaneously, in the same way that pencils and pens immediately mark paper as they are drawn over its surface, so the user has some feeling that the tool is being directly manipulated.

It was Ivan Sutherland's 'Sketchpad', of 1963, that first provided a practical way of making the paint system directly interactive by using a lightpen. Since then, most modern paint systems have abandoned this in favour of the stylus and digitizer, or the mouse. Recent developments include sophisticated, general-purpose software techniques that simulate traditional media from oil paint, watercolour and gouache, to pencil, charcoal and pastel. Computer 'brushes' can be dipped into water and then into the watercolour box, to create traditional watercolour effects. Overpainting and transparency are now standard options, and in the more expensive systems a pressure-sensitive stylus allows brush sizes to be increased or decreased with hand control.

While these techniques begin to exploit the capabilities of the computer, they also move it further away from the original painting metaphor, as the computer becomes an active partner rather than a passive toolbox. One major aspect of this third-generation computer paint tool, which sets it apart from the earlier, transitional tool, is its ability to simulate all traditional techniques by compressing them into one piece of software. This form of 'meta-tool' goes back to Turing's concept of the computer as a universal machine capable of simulating anything that can be written as a program.

How successful this new tool is, and how well the original painting metaphor has been interpreted and exceeded, is a matter for debate, but the fact is that, today, the computer paint system is a ubiquitous tool available to all designers and artists.

Two-dimensional Drawing

Many early attempts to use computers in an artistic context focused on getting the machine to produce a line drawing, so that work produced by the machine imitated work produced by hand. It is no accident that the computer plotter, which could draw lines on paper with a pen, was one early form of computer output. Much of this early work tended to be developed by computer scientists, and the few artists who were involved tended to start from a similar position, exploiting mathematically based techniques that were well suited to the computer, such as deformation and transformation. Formulae were keyed into the computer, which would then calculate a set of values and display the result as an image. Any aesthetic quality the visualized descriptions or formulae might have was purely accidental. The role of the artists was to take the original formulae and

Computer line drawings, either free or more geometric, were the first type of visual output. At this early stage the main attachment to the computer was the pen-plotter, which produced monochromatic line images with no areas of tone; coloured line work was only possible if coloured pens were put in the plotter. While this may now seem a serious constraint on creative endeavour, the range and quality of the work produced is quite surprising. The technique was most suitable for those who leaned towards a conceptual approach, and who could take advantage of the machine's stringent limitations, while exploiting its ability to produce multiple images at great speed. The image shown here was created by Colette and Charles Bangert in 1977.

Many artists worked on visual structures that transformed one object into another, thus taking advantage of the computer's skill at working out transformations in small, incremental stages. In this Japanese example, the computer constructs a series of forms that move between a square and a face, and then back to a square.

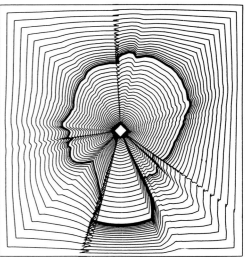

Another rich source of imagery was the scientific community, who began to see some aesthetic quality in the images they were producing. This sample, based on the neutron distribution in a rector, was produced by the Westinghouse Electric Corporation.

develop their artistic potential, deliberately looking for visual stimulus and trying to extract as much aesthetic quality as possible.

In the USA, Charles Csuri's pen plots of curved surfaces, based on boundary curves, were one example of this approach. Objects providing a simple profile that could be rotated became popular, and so the bottle and wine glass entered the vocabulary of computer graphics. Transformations of one object into another with all the 'in-between' stages was another favoured technique that suited early computer graphics systems.

All this work depended on the artist being able to program and to write the computer code that would generate the various permutations the image was required to undergo. This algorithmic approach (or as Herbert Franke calls it, 'calculation graphics'),[8] epitomised most early computer-generated line work. The early work used a black line on white paper, and the restrictions imposed by the plotting devices meant that there were severe limitations on what was possible.

The major difference between manual line work and computer-generated work was that the latter was produced by a set of programmed instructions that, in some senses, had little direct connection with the result. Lines of code were written and formulae embedded in the software, and the computer did the calculations, providing instructions to the plotter about where to draw the lines. This distancing of instruction from action, through the machine, introduced a radically new approach to image-making and challenged traditional notions of the role of the artist and designer. It was an approach later picked up by Harold Cohen (see pp. 130–1).

While the plotter was being used to output line work, the teletype machine was used to generate type, and it was not long before artists began to look to this machine as a means of creating images with words. Here was a new and unique form of visual expression, because it could not have happened without the invention of the computer and the teletype machine.

The work of Leon Harmon and Kenneth Knowlton stands out as particularly important in this short-lived area of imagery, which was to become debased through being hung on every office wall in the data-processing departments of the 1970s. The reclining nude (above right), produced for the Bell Laboratories, is probably the best-known example of such work. It is made up from separate letters and numbers, each of which corresponds to an average level of brightness, as computed for each unit of the original image (see pp. 14–15). Commenting on the work, Jasia Reichardt says 'What is interesting here is that neither Knowlton nor Harmon sought an image that would be either abstract or synthetic ... they considered that a common recognizable image (nude, gulls, gargoyle) would be the best vehicle to demonstrate the technique.... On the other hand, their aim was also to produce something in the idiom of modern art.'[9]

Simulated relief patterns resulted from a technique developed at MIT, which used data recorded by a television camera, processed in a computer and displayed on a high-resolution oscilloscope. This work by Efraim Arazi has a rich complexity and is remarkable for its visual quality.

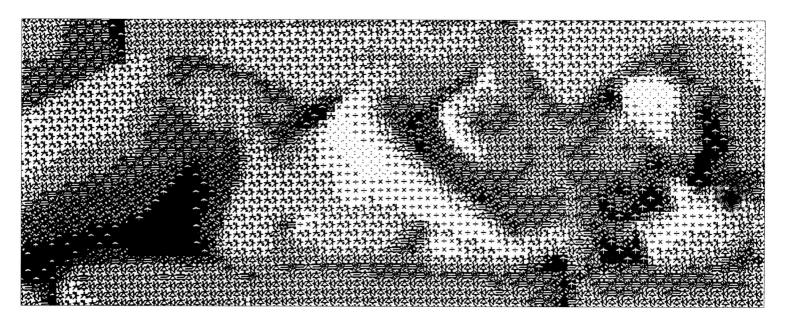

This form of computer drawing had little or no effect on contemporary artistic theory, but it marks a significant departure in the field of computer drawing. It was a milestone in the first, and largely misunderstood, decade of computer imagery.

The other, less artistic, result of two-dimensional computer graphics was the development of the technical drawing. Many large manufacturing companies, which produced vast quantities of technical drawings by hand, saw in the computer a means of rationalizing and automating their production. Just as the paint systems mimic the techniques of painting, so technical drawing systems copy handdrawn technical drawing methods, with the drawing sheet being retained as the basic form. In other words, the computer-generated technical drawing is just the digital equivalent of the paper drawing.

Of all the computer-based aids to design, the drafting system has become the most widely used in design offices, mainly because it does not challenge existing working methods and is highly productive. Architectural and engineering companies throughout the world have installed such systems as a first move in computerizing the design process – often with great success (see Chapter Three).

These drafting systems offer a series of menu options of basic forms. The drawings are composed of elements such as lines, circles, squares, triangles and arcs. The computer does not 'understand' what the drawing is – it is just a series of coordinates – but recent developments have provided some limited 'intelligence', so that the user gets feedback from the machine. There is no doubt that as more 'smart' techniques are applied to the computer-based technical drawing process, it will become increasingly linked into three-dimensional modelling. This will inevitably change the nature of the two-dimensional technical drawing, and may, perhaps, even see its demise as an isolated design activity.

The most famous of the Knowlton and Harmon works was the nude. Constructed in the same way as the others in the series (see p. 15), it was displayed as a 4-metre (12-ft) mural in the offices of the Bell Laboratories. Such images may be seen as employing visual techniques similar to those of Pointillist painting.

Three-dimensional Modelling

The artist's and designer's ability to create has not always been confined to a two-dimensional surface. Three-dimensional work has been a major form of expression in both fine art and design; in this context, drawing is confined to a subsidiary role and employed only as a means to an end. Three-dimensional objects have also dominated the crafts, and, latterly, engineering and architecture, with models and maquettes used for scaled-down or full-size representation.

The physical model, in both art and design, plays an important part in the development, presentation and storage of an idea. In the development stage, the model has to be capable of rapid change and not simply a way of storing the design idea in three-dimensional form. It is very important that alterations and variations can be made easily; the model must not constrain the design process simply because of the time and energy expended in its making. If this is the case, it can militate against the ability of the model to absorb adaptations. It is conceivable that the very quality of the final design and the efficiency of the product could depend on the ease with which the physical model can be adapted.

The role of the physical model as a storage medium was central to the architecture of the Baroque. In the late seventeenth century Sir Christopher Wren was asked to provide a design for the new St Paul's Cathedral in London, to 'be built according to a particular design of which the King did especially approve', a design that was to be recorded 'as a perpetual and unchanging rule in a wooden model'.[10] It was to be called the 'Great Model' – which indeed it was, as it took two years to build. However, it was superseded by other designs even before it was finished.

Using a model to 'store' the design was standard practice on projects that would take longer than the lifetime of the architect or patron to construct. It was one way of ensuring that large-scale constructional schemes would be completed as originally intended. But as construction time decreased, with techniques developed during the Industrial Revolution, the role of the constructional drawing increased. The division of labour into separate trades meant there was less need to build a large single model containing both structural and aesthetic information. With the introduction of computing, however, the idea of the large single model – the electronic database – is now regaining favour.

Nevertheless, the physical model is still very common in the motor car industry, for example, where the construction of clay models to describe complex curves is an integral part of the automobile designer's work. Drawings are often inadequate to describe the effect of the total shape of a car. The clay model not only allows for small design alterations, but eventually conveys to the client the full form of the final design, complete

'The Great Model' was made to represent the design for St Paul's Cathedral in London, proposed by the architect Sir Christopher Wren and agreed by a warrant from Charles II. It was intended to be a permanent record of the design, in case of accident to the architect, and to provide a clearer picture of the building to be constructed than could ever be captured by drawings. It could be walked through at eye level to replicate the experience of the interior in as realistic manner as was possible in those days. Costing about £600, it was completed in August 1674.

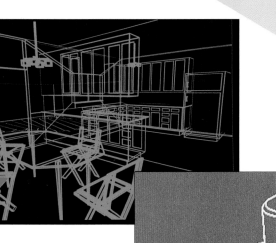

Wireframe construction (left) has been widely used as a technique in the making of three-dimensional computer models. Ivan Sutherland's 'Sketchpad' used this technique, and few attempts have been made since to search for alternatives. In the case of very complex objects, a wireframe representation can be very confusing. The technique of 'hidden-line removal' (centre) was developed to simplify the image by removing all those lines and surfaces that are hidden by others. The effect of these tools has been the challenge to create a photorealistic quality that displays the sophistication of the new software techniques. Examples like

the one on the right are now commonplace, as software companies strive to show how their latest ray-traced images can simulate reality. Visual artists have often sought to capture a realistic image of reality – the Dutch painters of the seventeenth century, for example, and more recently the Photorealism movement in painting. However, many consider this goal an aesthetic dead-end.

These illustrations represent three-dimensional modelling of a very sophisticated kind. The first image (left), developed for a television series on Mongolia, is an accurate reconstruction of a thirteenth-century castle in Dadu (now Beijing). The next (below) is a rendering for eye glasses, while the car image (right) is constructed against the background of a Parisian night scene. The final illustration (inset, right) is a fashion design simulation developed in Japan.

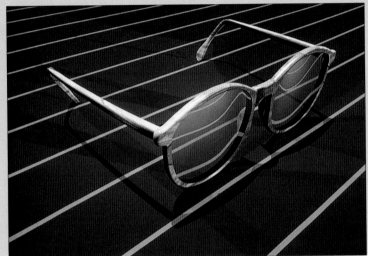

with all the subtle patterns of light and shade that are such an important factor in the marketing of a car.

Early three-dimensional computer systems displayed simple shapes by tracing outlines of all the edges, forming an often ambiguous 'wireframe' image. However, as the objects displayed become more complex the viewer had great difficulty in understanding the images; software was therefore written that removed a line if it was hidden behind another line. The convincing representation of solid surfaces was the next breakthrough. And so three-dimensional modelling systems began the climb to the level of photorealistic representation that is seen today.

The perspective techniques that had been used for centuries to provide the illusion of depth were transcribed into the computer system – but there was one drawback. When a painter uses perspective to create an impression of depth, no matter how realistic the impression, if the painting is turned around the object or scene depicted does not appear on the back. The illusion is essentially contained on the surface. The difficulty of describing three-dimensional objects proved a central problem in the development of modelling software for the computer.

The computer was required to close the gap between reality and the illusion displayed on a two-dimensional surface. In order to do this, it had to 'understand' fully in three dimensions, otherwise it would not know what to do when asked for a different view of the object. The artist only needed to make the object look real from one angle, but the computer database had to simulate all the dimensional properties of the real object. This problem – like many others – was solved at the University of Utah in the early 1970s.

Once the major breakthrough had occurred, a second issue became clear. This was the realization that there was a significant difference between the way the three-dimensional image was stored in the database of the computer, and the way in which it was to be displayed. In the computer, the model was made up of edges, their size and relationships. The display of the object was concerned not only with this, but also with the position of the viewer, who controlled the perspective of the object, the lighting, texture and scale.

In looking at a physical model, viewers are not fully aware of the complexity of the relationships within an object. They stand at a certain distance from it, at a certain angle to it, so that only certain aspects of it show. As they move around, other views are seen; if more detail is needed, they move closer, while moving away provides them with a more general view. All of this is normal behaviour when viewing a model, and, most importantly, it occurs as a series of unconscious acts. It is so much part of everyday experience that, when looking at an object, viewers are not aware of their spatial relationship with the model in anything like these terms.

However, when the real-world situation is translated into computing terms, all these factors have to be calculated to establish the same kind of three-dimensional readings that are normally expected. The difference is that, when using a computer, the calculation has to be driven by conscious choice. The user has to decide exactly what the spatial relationship is between him- or herself and the object.

This is what makes three-dimensional computer modelling often so complex. Not only does the design model have to be built in terms very different from its physical counterpart, but information that is normally assumed has to be consciously supplied. In addition, the physical model has other characteristics, such as surface texture and the effect of light. If these are added – as they must be to reinforce the realism of the computer-generated image – then the situation is further complicated.

In spite of its complexity, the three-dimensional computer model is becoming an impressive and powerful new tool. When used effectively, it can provide a new relationship between designers who think in three dimensions – architects, interior designers, industrial designers – and their designs.

Hypertext and Hypercard

Other new tools have emerged that do not reflect past traditions, but have their genesis in a more general computer framework. The most striking of these tools, which have only

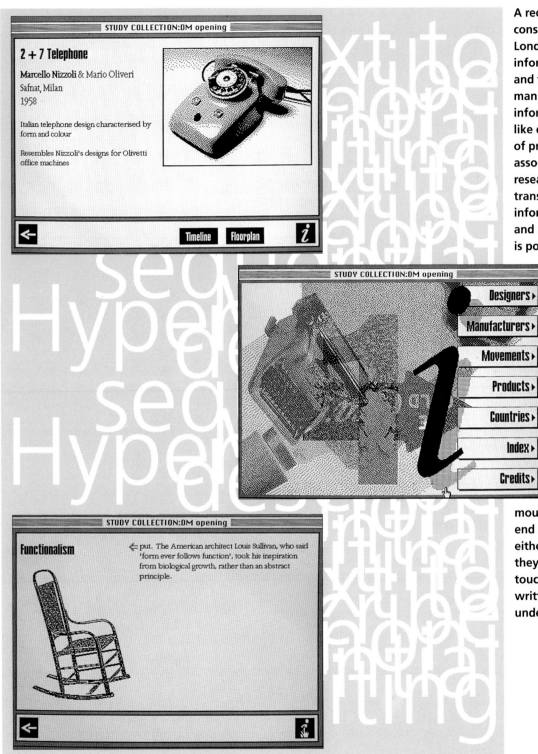

STUDY COLLECTION:DM opening

2 + 7 Telephone

Marcello Nizzoli & Mario Oliveri
Safnat, Milan
1958

Italian telephone design characterised by form and colour

Resembles Nizzoli's designs for Olivetti office machines

Timeline | Floorplan | *i*

STUDY COLLECTION:DM opening

Designers ▸
Manufacturers ▸
Movements ▸
Products ▸
Countries ▸
Index ▸
Credits ▸

STUDY COLLECTION:DM opening

Functionalism

put. The American architect Louis Sullivan, who said 'form ever follows function', took his inspiration from biological growth, rather than an abstract principle.

A recent use of Hypercard is the database constructed for the Design Museum in London. This allows visitors to look up information about the objects on display and the background to their design and manufacture. The various pieces of information are connected by links, which, like electronic footnotes, point the reader of printed matter to related points, associated topics and areas for further research. The links within Hypercard transport the user around the network of information, making it more manageable and more responsive to individual needs. It is possible to opt for a predetermined path, constructed by someone else, or to select your own path – or to combine the two. With these methods users can quickly browse through large stacks of information, finding out what is important to them. The screen-sized cards are organized into topic-related stacks, and as each card is displayed, text and graphics can be created in the same way as on other Macintosh software. The associative link between the cards is provided by buttons, which are activated by clicking with the mouse; this brings up the card at the other end of the association. The buttons can be either text or graphics, and if necessary they can be completely invisible. The touching of a button executes a script written in HyperTalk, which is the underlying programming language.

just begun to exert their influence on design, is 'Hypertext'. Ted Nelson, an early American visionary in this area of work, coined the word 'Hypertext' some twenty-five years ago to describe nonsequential writing. Nelson has since begun work on the enormous task of devising an on-line network of the world's literary treasures, called 'Xanadu'. This project, which is perhaps the best-known use of a Hypertext system, provides a vision of the literary database of the future. By accessing Xanadu, you can browse literary works, select and compare texts, and then connect up digitally with a range of other media, including relevant films or television programmes, for example.

Hypertext systems now come in many guises, but the most familiar are the 'Guide' software, which runs mainly on the IBM personal computer, and 'Hypercard', on the Apple Macintosh. Hypercard, created by Bill Atkinson of Apple, uses the metaphor of the index card as a way of storing information on computer. Hypercard is not really an application, like word-processing or a spreadsheet, but is more of a tool kit, which can be used to create and customize information. At its most basic level Hypercard is a database management system that lets you connect screens of information using associative links.

Structure and the New Tools

The art historian has provided many systems for the analysis of paintings and drawings, in an attempt to interpret the underlying structure of works of art. Attempts to grasp this structure have focused on how paintings and buildings were constructed according to rules of geometric composition and proportion. The Golden Mean, for example, provided a canonical system of aesthetic organization over many centuries.

Eminent Victorians sought to discover the rules used for the construction of the Gothic cathedrals in northern Europe, as a way of trying to understand the governing principles that had structured the work of the original stonemasons. During the early twentieth century, the French architect Le Corbusier reintroduced the concept of a proportional system for visual organization. More recently, ideas have emerged from psychology – particularly the psychology of visual perception – as a richer source of explanation. Rudolf Arnheim's contribution to the interpretation of art was largely devoted to suggesting a set of such ordering systems. In *The Power of the Centre*,[11] he analyses Matisse's painting *Gourds* and concludes 'The various structural principles overlay one another and frequently endow a particular element with contradictory characteristics and functions, making it at once central and peripheral, strong and weak, detached and connected.'

However, when structure is talked about in connection with the new computer tools, a rather different concept is involved. Structure in a computer-generated drawing is not only concerned with the compositional values mentioned by Arnheim and others, but with a further dimension that is not present in traditional works.

An early example of the implicit structure that later became a characteristic of electronic images is a woven silk portrait of J.M. Jacquard, inventor of the Jacquard loom.

A LA MÉMOIRE DE J. M. JACQUARD.

Nineteenth-century woven silk portrait of the inventor of the Jacquard loom. The detail above reveals the underlying structure, 'programmed' into the loom by means of punched cards.

His loom used punched paper cards that carried detailed information about the pattern to be woven. When the cards were fed into the loom as a continuous strip, the information was 'read' by the loom, and translated into the design, with the machine selecting the correct threads and colours. The portrait of Jaquard (left), woven in 1854, was constructed exactly in this manner. The image was coded onto punched cards – which formed the structure behind the image – enabling the loom to interpret the intention of the designer. Clearly it would have been possible to create any number of identical images from the cards.

Much later Ivan Sutherland describes what he feels to be the advantage of the computer drawing over the hand drawing: 'To a large extent it has turned out that the usefulness of computer drawings is precisely their structured nature.... An ordinary [designer] is unconcerned with the structure of his drawing material. Pen and ink or pencil and paper have no inherent structure. They only make dirty marks on paper. The [designer] is concerned principally with the drawings as a representation of the evolving design. The behaviour of the computer-produced drawings, on the other hand, is critically dependent upon the topological and geometric structure built up in the computer memory as a result of drawing operations. The drawing itself has properties quite independent of the object it is describing.'[12]

If there is one major difference between the old tools and the new, it probably has to do with this concept. What distinguishes the new technologies from traditional techniques is the ability to generate other kinds of information about various processes beyond the operation of the original process itself. In the supermarket, for example, computer-controlled checkout systems are designed to total a customer's purchases. They not only do this, but can also provide details on stock levels, customer preferences and purchasing profile, which, if fed back into the system, can generate information for a variety of analytic functions.

The fundamental duality of the new tools, as Shoshana Zuboff explains, has not been fully appreciated. 'On the one hand, the technology can be applied to automating operations according to a logic that hardly differs from that of the nineteenth-century machine system – replace the human body with a technology that enables the same processes to be performed with more continuity and control. On the other, the same technology simultaneously generates information about the underlying productive and administrative processes through which an organization accomplishes its work. It provides a deeper level of transparency to activities that had been either partially or completely opaque.'[13]

What is the effect on the kind of computing used by artists and designers? The duality is largely unplanned and often unrecognized, so the opportunity to use it creatively is still wide open. It is therefore up to the art and design community to see how this potential might be directed towards a humanistic purpose.

Point of sale computer which records not only the transactions with the public but uses that information to form the basis of a number of analyses that including buying preferences, stock control and other administrative and marketing tasks.

3 TRANSFORMING THE PRESENT

During the 1980s most art and design disciplines were exposed to some form of computerization. The application of computing has been slow and intermittent, but certain disciplines can now provide examples of best practice that others could learn from. The 1980s will thus be remembered as the decade when computers firmly established their position in the commercial fields of art and design.

Today, it is difficult to find a design office that does not use a computer system for creative work in one context or another. In art and design educational institutions, too, there is now sufficient experience for staff to understand the implications of using computing within their disciplines. Students graduating over the last two decades have had practical experience in the use of computer tools; many have gone on to gain influential positions in design organizations, where they have invested in the technology.

This chapter provides a survey of how the use of computing has developed in the various art and design disciplines. The intention is to offer an overview of the changes that are occurring, by emphasizing the significant effects of the introduction of the new technologies. For example, the computer has encouraged the gradual, but inevitable, merging of previously separate disciplines. Although each discipline is discussed individually in this chapter, the boundaries between the disciplines are in fact becoming increasingly blurred. It is interesting to explore the implications of this merging process for both the content of design and the nature of the new designer.

Broadly speaking, computing has been applied to design and the visual arts in two ways, and it is possible to find examples of both approaches in the universities, colleges and design offices of Europe, the United States, Australia and Japan.

On the one hand, computing is seen as playing a supporting role that underpins all the other disciplines; in this case, it is seen as a tool. In the hands of an artist or designer, the computer can be used to visualize ideas and to provide instructions for making objects in areas as diverse as fashion, textiles, industrial design, architecture, interior design, ceramics, film, photography, video, graphic design, painting, printmaking and sculpture. In these disciplines, the new technologies tend to operate in parallel with traditional techniques.

Alternatively, computing may be considered as a topic in its own right that should be taught as a major subject, like painting, graphic design or interior design. This is the position now taken by most educational institutions, and progressive design organizations, certainly in the United States, are beginning to experiment with developing aspects of computing as a commercial design discipline.

Currently, use of computers falls largely within the first category, and the examples that follow establish the extent to which the new technologies have penetrated a variety of disciplines. The interesting question that arises is: what aspects of their content are appropriate for computing? And this leads us to consider to what extent these areas can remain viable, in terms of content and meaning, as isolated and separate disciplines.

Computing has been integrated into the design disciplines in a fragmented fashion, because only in recent times have the four major conditions for this development been in place. These provide the basis for the computer to become a ubiquitous tool that will aid, rather than obscure, the process of design.

First – and of major significance – there was the development of the Graphical User Interface (GUI), which relies on a visual, rather than a purely numerical or textual representation of information. It allows designers, who come from a predominately visual culture, to apply some of their original skills to computing, without the need to learn an entirely new language. There were instances of computers being applied within industrial design and architectural practices well before the availability of the GUI, but, while such practices proved useful trailblazers, enabling a great deal to be learnt from their pioneering efforts, much scepticism was expressed about the relevance of computer tools to design. Their seemingly 'alien' procedures created within the design community an attitude of suspicion, concerning the machine's threat to creativity. This attitude still exists in some backwaters of the design profession.

The second major breakthrough was the introduction of the pen and mouse. Designers were never fully convinced that the keyboard was an appropriate tool with which to communicate with a machine. Many put up with it, as they did not realize that there might be an alternative. More importantly, they did not feel it was their responsibility to improve the situation. The pen and mouse demonstrated how the method and form of interaction might be considerably improved. Again, this development allowed designers to see a link with traditional design skills.

Thirdly, cost was a significant factor in the uptake of computing in many areas of commerce – and so it was to be in design. From the standpoint of design organizations, hardware and software were very expensive; they had not been used to making high capital investments, except in property. The tools that they traditionally used – the range of workshop tools, for example – were not only low in cost, but their function and role

The Empire Strikes Back (1977) was an early example of the potential of the new technology to transform the cinema. Animated sequences were used to enhance the live, filmed action.

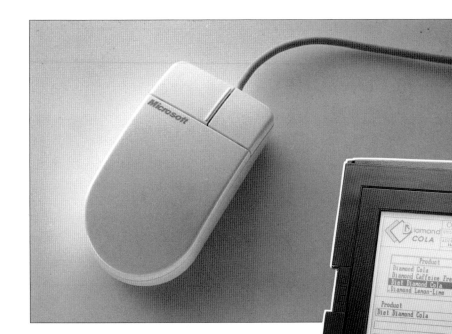

For designers, as for lay users, new ways of interacting with the computer have not been restricted to the computer screen; they have spread to the hardware. The mouse, designed to be used with the Graphical User Interface, represented a new way of directing the computer – by pointing and clicking. Although the mouse replaced many functions, it did not replace the keyboard. Users have had to wait until the early 1990s for a new range of computers where the keyboard has been entirely displaced by the pen or stylus.

were very clear-cut. Initially, therefore, it was only the larger, more profitable, practices that began to introduce computing. However, the computer became a much more widespread tool as costs dropped, allowing smaller design companies, which make up by far the largest section of the design community, to make purchases.

The fourth condition for the adoption of computing by designers was met when appropriate design-orientated, low-cost, easy-to-use software began to be made available. Once all these preconditions were in place, the design community could begin to understand the basis of the new design practice.

The rest of this chapter explores how the computer is used as a tool in design and art disciplines. The brief commentary on each discipline is supported by captioned illustrations that provide working examples. Although each commentary deals with a particular discipline, issues raised in connection with one discipline may well apply to several others, as the barriers between the 'watertight' compartments of traditional design thinking begin to break down in the new electronic environment.

Industrial Design

As in the case of other design disciplines, computing was first applied to industrial design in an attempt to automate existing work practices and skills. Software used in design practices enabled the computerization of the two-dimensional technical drawing and the

The laptop computer is not just another computer, but without a keyboard; it is an entirely fresh concept: an electronic notebook with an electronic pen. It is strange that the words notebook and pen should survive into the electronic era, but as the technology advances, designers are trying to integrate natural and intuitive ways of doing things into electronic products.

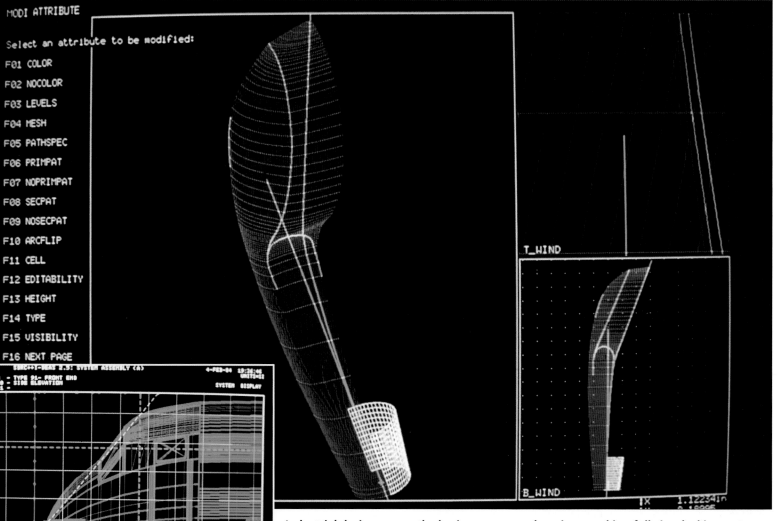

MODI ATTRIBUTE

Select an attribute to be modified:

F01 COLOR
F02 NOCOLOR
F03 LEVELS
F04 MESH
F05 PATHSPEC
F06 PRIMPAT
F07 NOPRIMPAT
F08 SECPAT
F09 NOSECPAT
F10 ARCFLIP
F11 CELL
F12 EDITABILITY
F13 HEIGHT
F14 TYPE
F15 VISIBILITY
F16 NEXT PAGE

T_WIND

B_WIND

Industrial designers use the basic conventions of the technical drawing to convey information to the manufacturer. The instructions must be clear, unambiguous and easily understood by the recipient. Such drawings are an obvious candidate for computerization, and most early computer systems used in the profession were able to produce technical drawings. Although the computer drawings look like their hand-drawn predecessors, they are more than just electronic copies of the manual process. The concept of the master drawing, and functions such as layering, working full-size, locking onto grids and automatic dimensioning, are only possible in the electronic version.

Making models in a computer involves a very different process from building them physically. The computer designs the object using a wireframe model, which is given surface characteristics, such as colour and texture, at a later stage. As the concept of making a model out of numbers has become more familiar, the three-dimensional computer model has become the touchstone of many industrial design practices.

three-dimensional model – a development that demonstrated considerable savings in time and money.

Technical drawing was a manual process that was easily transferable to the electronic environment of the computer. As the drawing moved from the manual to the electronic, it took with it many drawing conventions, such as the use of drawing sheets, overlays, borders and variations in line thickness. Every effort was made to make the drawing appear as familiar as possible, so that users could feel the new technique was just an extension of manual paper practice.

This approach tended to cloud the advantages of the new electronic tools, which contained emerging concepts such as the 'pull-down' menu and the shared database; they allowed a high level of accuracy and the storing of full-size information. Once the information had been translated into digital form it could be used in many different ways. These aspects of the computer emerged slowly, as designers began to appreciate these

The physical model has always played an important role in the development of design ideas, particularly in industrial design, where it was difficult to gain a true impression of a three-dimensional design from a two-dimensional sketch. The model had an important tactile, as well as a visual role. According to the industrial designer's traditional working method, sketch models would be used as part of the design process, with a final presentation model being made to communicate the design to the client. Right: model of a TV/mirror.

alternatives to the manual model, which challenged the traditional conventions and role of the technical drawing.

Three-dimensional computer-based modelling shared some of the teething troubles apparent in the development of the computerized technical drawing. The role of 'hard' three-dimensional models in industrial design has a long history, so work practices have become intertwined with the modelling process to such an extent that it is often difficult to separate them. When first introduced, three-dimensional computer modelling was notoriously difficult – so much so, that many practices failed to take to it until very recently. Even when they did, many soon became dissatisfied with it as a design tool.

But things have changed since the early days, and many designers are beginning to see the advantages of the 'soft' model made from numbers, rather than clay or foam. Certainly, once the model has been built, the number of design iterations – of shape, texture and colour – that can be explored without incurring a great time penalty, is considerable. There are still difficulties with the interface and with the conceptual methods of computer modelling. Nevertheless, three-dimensional modelling is now integrated into many industrial design practices as a design tool.

The American computer graphics conference SIGGRAPH sponsored a competition for the most innovative form of computer-generated teapot design. Some of the results are shown above.

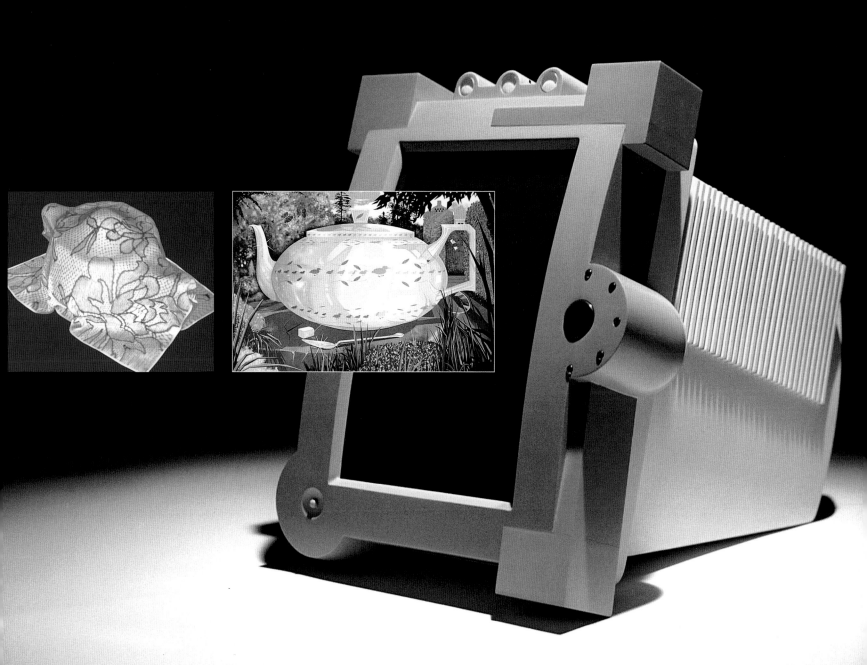

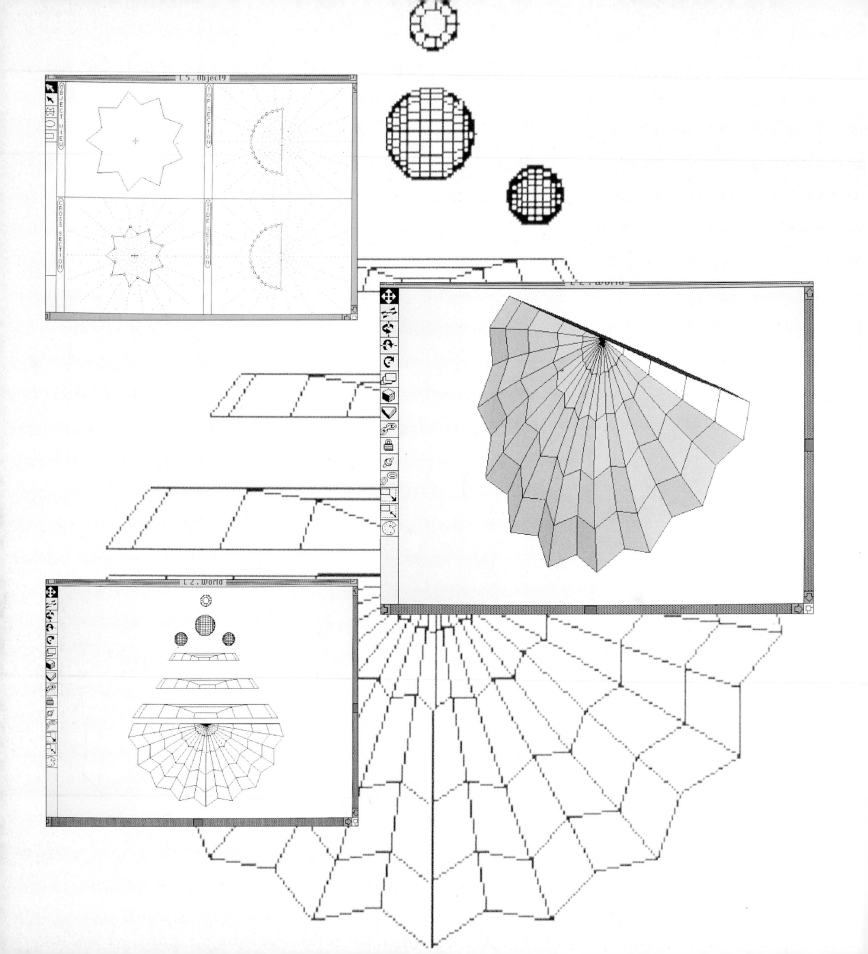

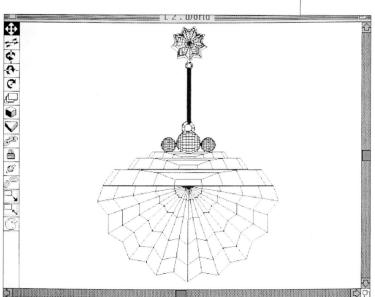

The new skills required for computer modelling are very different from those for building a physical model. To make best use of the computer model it is important to know how it can be constructed efficiently and without compromising the design intention. Knowledge of numerical models is essential to understand fully how the various component forms are made and assembled. The illustrations shown here give an impression of what it is like to use a very simple modelling package on the Macintosh computer. They show the various stages in preparing a design for a pair of earrings.

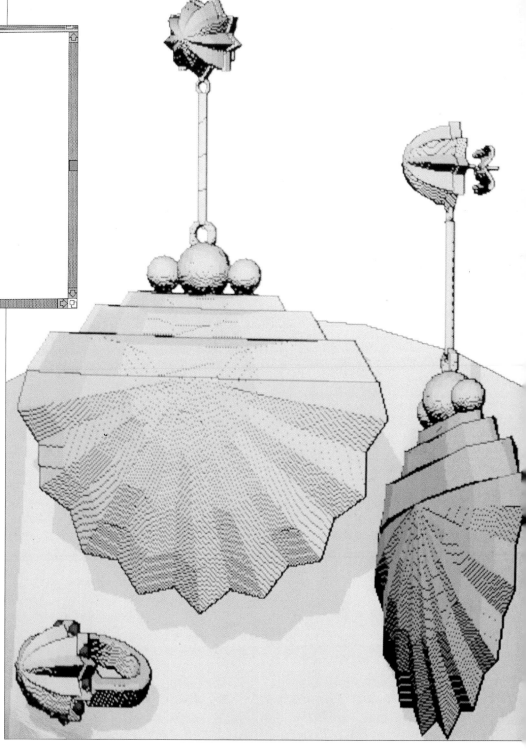

The future of modelling techniques lies in the ability not only to visualize the three-dimensional design of a product, but to simulate how that product works. This can be interpreted in two ways. It may involve studying how the intended user will react to the product, or, on a more technical level, examining the design from a production point of view. In the first context, three-dimensional modelling software would be used to make the model, and then animation software would make the product perform all the intended functions. This would not only give users insight into the design of the object; it would also enable them to appreciate how it would look and feel in use.

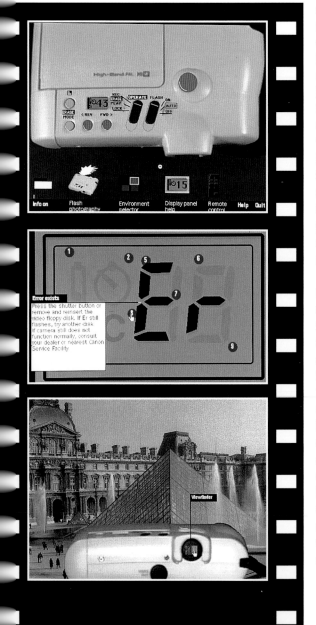

Computer models can be made that simulate not only the visual characteristics of a product, but also how it works. These illustrations (left) show a scanned-in image of a video still camera, on which all the buttons are active and behave as the real buttons would. The view through the viewfinder is also shown, so that the 'photographer' can see the picture that is being taken. The numerical indicator shows the number of shots that have been taken and advances after each shot; the camera flash is operated when the take button is pressed. This product already exists, but clearly it would have been possible to simulate it before it was produced.

Computer-aided modelling systems have tried to mimic the physical process, but they are probably more effective for producing final images than working constructs. Even the new generation of 'designer' modellers still require quite precise, detailed information to create a computer model. This need for accuracy frequently conflicts with the initial stages of the design process, because ambiguity and imprecision are often the very hallmarks of creativity. In spite of this, computer modelling systems are becoming a standard tool in the industrial design studio, as the advantages of an electronic model become more obvious and begin to challenge traditional working procedures. Right: three-dimensional computer model of a hi-fi unit.

In a more technical context, once the digital model were complete, the information could be used to test the strength of the materials, and indicate, for example, how a molten material might flow in a mould. This ability to see how objects will 'work' could be of distinct advantage to designers as they strive to make products cheaper, to improve quality and cut down the time required to get a product on to the market.

However, optimization – as this process has been called – should not be restricted to providing stress analysis and mould flow information. It should also have an impact on other aspects of a design and its performance, such as the choice of materials, issues of form, and eventually, user concerns. At present, computational analysis verifies the product geometry, rather than offering refined formal options or user alternatives. General-purpose optimization techniques with both analytic and design sensitivity are required; these could then be integrated into a range of design tools. Most importantly, such optimization techniques constitute a background activity that is transparent to the designer. Thus, optimization, in its broadest sense, forms part of a larger and more sophisticated computer-based toolkit.

Optimization provides the basis for an industrial design version of concurrent engineering, which will contribute to shorter lead-times and quality design solutions. Economic recession has placed such tools in a far more strategic position, from which they will increasingly affect the nature and role of industrial design. Computing will probably prove the only means of enabling industrial designers to meet their clients' requirements for ever finer design optimization. Just as it is now impossible to conceive of designing an aircraft or a car without a computer, before long it will be inconceivable to design even quite small products without the aid of the machine.

It is not only the tools that are beginning to look different; what the designer does is also beginning to change. While industrial designers will still need to work on a range of familiar consumer products, at the boundaries of traditional expertise disciplines are emerging that require the development of new skills. The need to form working liaisons with other disciplines – some of which may have little connection with design – is going to be an important consideration for the future.

Interaction design (see p. 143), one of the crossover disciplines that are beginning to appear, involves the study of how users interact with computers and other electronic consumer products. This has always been a substratum of industrial design, but it is undoubtedly now becoming a discipline in its own right, incorporating aspects of cognitive psychology, of design and of human behaviour. Such trends are shifting the balance away from the product and towards the process. In so doing, they are redefining the boundaries of what is called industrial design.

Computer models still do not solve the problem of touch and feel. When virtual reality becomes commonplace, however, this could become a simulated option, so that it would be possible, for example, to wear this sun watch and sense how it feels.

One advantage of the computer model is that the information used to construct it can be employed for other purposes. Finite element analysis – testing to see where stresses will occur – was once a process in which designers did not participate. Now it is possible to simulate such an analysis on a desktop computer, with the result that the role of the industrial designer is being extended into new areas of competence. The analysis of how a liquid material will behave when poured into a mould (opposite, above and below left) is another example. It provides vital information about likely manufacturing problems, so the design can be changed before it has been finalized. Very few design practices currently exploit the full potential of their computer systems. The industrial design practice of the future could extend their role in this, and other directions, as clients increasingly seek optimum design solutions.

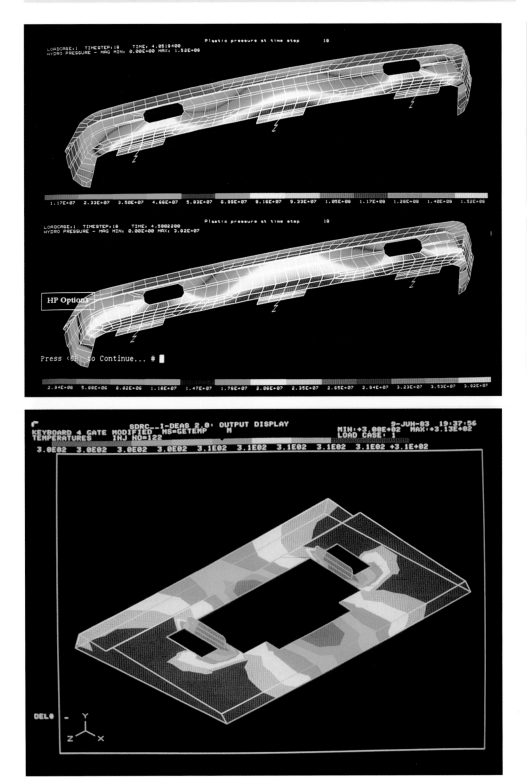

The American organization IDEO is a typical example of the new generation of industrial design practices. They are as yet few in number, but they are characterized by their expansion into new areas of design, such as interaction design. This nautical navigator (above) was not simply designed as a physical product; it included methods of interaction and screen layouts – another demonstration of how the designer's skill base is being extended.

Automobile Design

The automobile industry was one of the first to use computer-aided design systems. Considerable experience had already been gained in the use of computers to perform administrative and organizational tasks, and as the design and construction of cars had always required high capital investment, the scene was set for the introduction of computers as an engineering design tool. By the mid-1980s most of the world's larger car manufacturers had installed a computer design system and were beginning to recognize that it could design cars more efficiently than traditional methods.

However, the transition from manual to electronic methods was slow and fraught with difficulties. Early computer systems were designed to be very self-contained, resulting in 'islands of automation' with no electronic connection between them. This meant that the full benefits of computerization could not be established, because one major advantage of computerization is the ability to exchange information wherever and whenever necessary. Another problem was that car designers began to be recruited among design rather than engineering graduates, who in the early days had little or no computer experience. As a consequence, they did not really understand computer systems, nor did they consider them a useful tool. Even to this day, many automobile companies still run both traditional and computer systems side by side in their design departments. Perhaps there is something about the size, cost and complexity of the car that makes the transition from old to new methods especially difficult to resolve. This is apparent, for example, in the fact that huge, expensive and inaccurate clay models are still built, even though new software developments and the increasing ability of computers to 'talk' to each other does allow the complete design process to be undertaken within the electronic environment.

The new generation of computer modelling systems, produced with the designer in mind, does go some way towards providing more useful tools, which reveal some understanding of how designers work. Car designs can be constructed and then rendered to a level of visualization that would be very laborious to produce using manual methods, displaying all the surface characteristics – such as reflections – that would be expected in a typical car showroom. The quality and accuracy of such modellers allow designers to produce realistic images far beyond what could be achieved by hand.

However, one major fault with earlier modellers was that the information on the computer model, while sufficient to show how a car would look, was limited in its mathematical accuracy. To an extent, this has been corrected by the introduction into many modellers of a mathematical construct called NURBS (Non-Uniform Rational B Spline). This provides information about complex shapes in an efficient form that can be

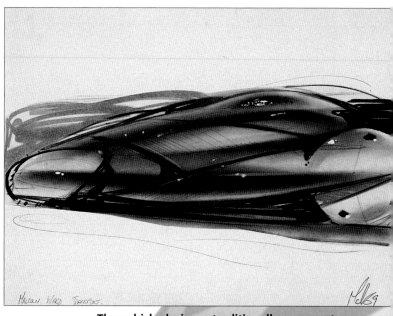

The vehicle designer traditionally uses a set of drawing and modelling tools that have been around for some time to make presentations of design ideas. The sketch (above) has become a highly stylized means for representing how light and shade fall on the complex, coloured surface of a car.

Right: a computer-generated concept for a car design using highlights. Some computer modellers can give an impression of reflections, to show the designer how various forms will look under different lighting conditions. The ever-increasing importance of styling, by which design is used as a marketing tool, is another essential aspect of the designer's role in the automobile industry.

used by numerically controlled machines. These can then manufacture the design, cutting it directly out of plastic foam at full size, thus avoiding the need to create the traditional clay model.

Such techniques begin to establish the advantages of modelling an object, rather than just recording it in a drawing. A model provides many types of useful, comprehensive information. A single, unambiguous representation of the design demonstrates, for example, how pieces fit together; whether there is a clash between components; and answers questions of cost and weight. Another advantage in something as complex as a car is that the single design model can be described at various levels of detail. In other words, the form in which the information is stored within the computer varies according to the data required for each particular design or engineering task. The centralized database contains the design in numerical form; from this can be extracted information that will aid maintenance, as well as providing engineering and design details to be used in manuals or to update the product later on. These advantages are already apparent in the aircraft industry, where a single design for an aircraft may contain about six million separate parts. The same techniques are now becoming commonplace within the automobile industry.

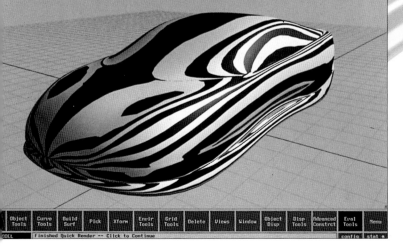

The major modelling technique employed in the car industry is still the traditional clay model (above), built first to one-fifth scale and finally full size. In spite of the cost and the difficulty in making changes to the clay model, it is still the most important way of assessing a design.

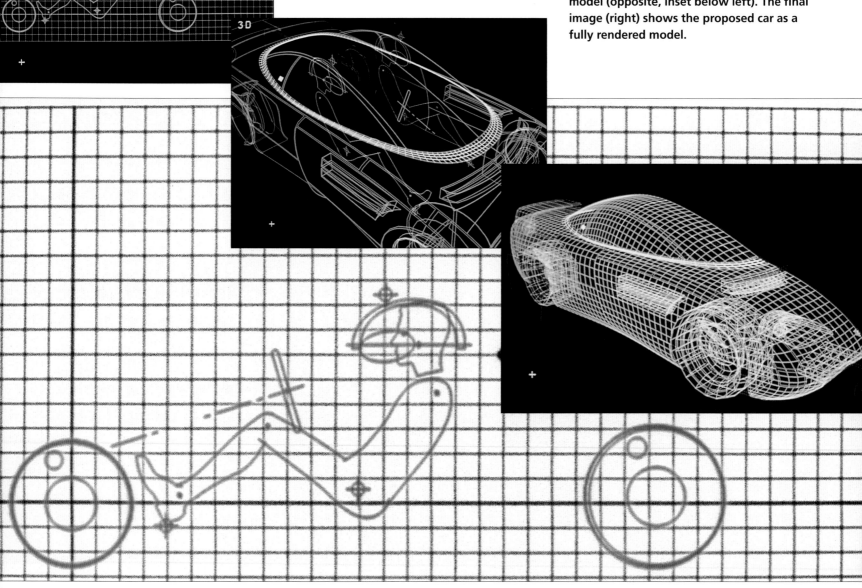

This series of images shows how a car design is developed using a computer system. The package drawing (left) contains the basic components. The next two images show how the outline surface is defined. The computer system then produces an image that simulates the traditional clay model (opposite, inset below left). The final image (right) shows the proposed car as a fully rendered model.

Almost every brochure sent out by the major software vendors who produce three-dimensional modellers includes a photograph of a fully rendered car. The surface of a car is very complex to model accurately; it requires powerful rendering software to achieve a photorealistic quality – an achievement that should not be underrated. The car has therefore become the ultimate test, so any self-respecting software package must have one. Right: computer-generated image of a car in a showroom, complete with simulated highlights.

One example of the kind of development that will determine the future use of CAD systems within the automobile industry is the Evans & Sutherland Computer Design and Rendering System (CDRS) – shown in use at the Royal College of Art above right (inset). It can be used to produce a series of computer models from a package drawing showing initial design constraints, a basic 'clay' model and a fully rendered version. Information from the database can also be used to drive a machine that cuts a full-size mock-up of the car design out of plastic foam (above).

Architecture

Computer tools supporting the design and construction of buildings have been in place for some time. Certainly in Europe and America, architectural firms and schools of architecture were among the first organizations to use the new technology. This early start, combined with the considerable theoretical tradition that has built up over the centuries, has resulted in theoretical, as well as practical developments in computer-aided architectural design.

Recent attempts at visual realism have used a software technique called ray-tracing, by which the computer traces every ray of light in a given image and represents it on the screen. This produces very sharp, precise images, which are often so crisp as to be unconvincing. Such photorealistic rendering has the disadvantage of taking up considerable computer time. Also, as the image is seen only from a specific viewpoint, other views cannot be shown unless the computer recalculates the entire image.

Theories of how architects work abound, but most traditional descriptions outline a series of steps spanning from the inception of the project, through sketch ideas to the final design scheme, and then to its implementation as a three-dimensional structure. While this description is useful in helping us to understand the sequential stages, it does not reflect the *type* of design involved. A new form of representation is needed to deal with the application of the new technologies to architecture and to other design disciplines. In this context, the classes of design outlined in Chapter One (p. 20) – routine, innovative and creative – may be useful.

It is interesting to see how these classes of design map on to the computer work currently being done within the architectural profession. Software enables users to construct and edit drawings, by using geometric primitives and libraries of classified parts to perform rendering tasks. Combined with three-dimensional modelling and viewing, these form the basis of most commercial CAD packages used in architecture today.

Much two-dimensional technical drawing – and some three-dimensional computer modelling – that fails to exploit any of the advantages of the computer could be seen as routine design work. However, the standard computer tools that can be found in current commercial software can also be used for innovative design work, allowing architectural ideas to be represented in a highly sophisticated visual manner. Detailed walk-throughs of virtual buildings, for example, are now commonplace; these exploit the computer's characteristically tireless ability to produce accurately rendered interior perspectives. Experimental concepts such as shape grammars (see p. 171) are also innovative procedures that may well have a future in commercial CAD packages. Designers could use such techiques to generate designs by working with sophisticated structures and rules, rather than simply manipulating geometric primitives.

Representational modelling of building interiors has reached a level of realism that allows the exploration of design ideas at a precise level. Walls, floors, ceilings and all the interior fitments can be modelled in full colour and texture, so that clients can get a feeling of exactly how the design will look. Interior lighting and daylight are now well understood, and highly accurate computer programs exist that can produce a convincing rendering. Left and right: architectural rendering of an office interior.

Radiosity provides a much softer image than ray-tracing. It calculates the entire three-dimensional environment, independently of the viewpoint, so that it can support fly-through scenes. The theatre auditorium shown left was modelled in mid-1991 by a San Francisco firm of architects for a proposed new building in the city. At that time it was the most complex radiosity solution

ever computed. Radiosity could prove a very usable rendering technique for architects and designers. The domestic interior of the piano room in North Carolina (inset, below left) was modelled in Autocad; the radiosity technique was then applied. Above: interior created with an architectural rendering program called Zero One.

Many of the realistic images shown in computer magazines display the full functionality of a software product. However, these are often computed as part of the research programme undertaken by the software house. Many of the packages are in fact laborious to learn and require a high level of computer science skills to extract the desired result. Fortunately, this position is changing as the gap between software user and software producer narrows. The interior (right), designed by a group of Cincinnati architects, is an interesting example of an image taken from the computer screen and reproduced as a silkscreen print, with all the surfaces and shadows treated as flat tones.
Inset: model of the interior of a boiler room.

It is not just the creation of new buildings that is in the minds of architects when they use computer modelling systems, but also the re-creation of historic buildings. Such an approach is particularly relevant at a time when the profession is leaning stylistically on the past for its preferred solutions. Many important expressions of the modern movement in architecture can now be viewed as computer models. Above: computer-modelled interior of a basilica. Above right: interior of Le Corbusier's chapel at Ronchamp in south-eastern France. Right: interior of Chartres cathedral.

The London architects GMW make extensive use of computer systems, as this model of a proposed design for Mappin Terraces at London Zoo indicates. It creates an exciting backdrop for the animals.

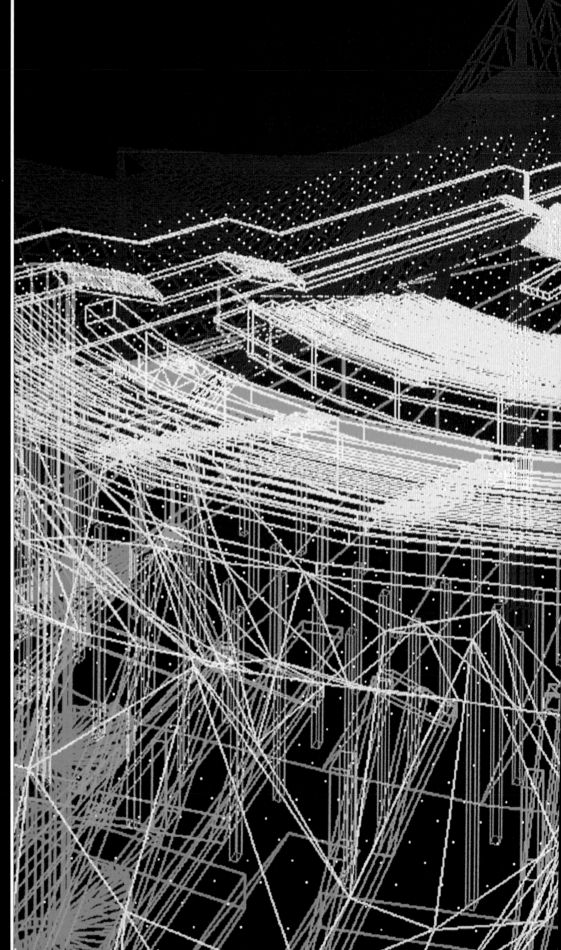

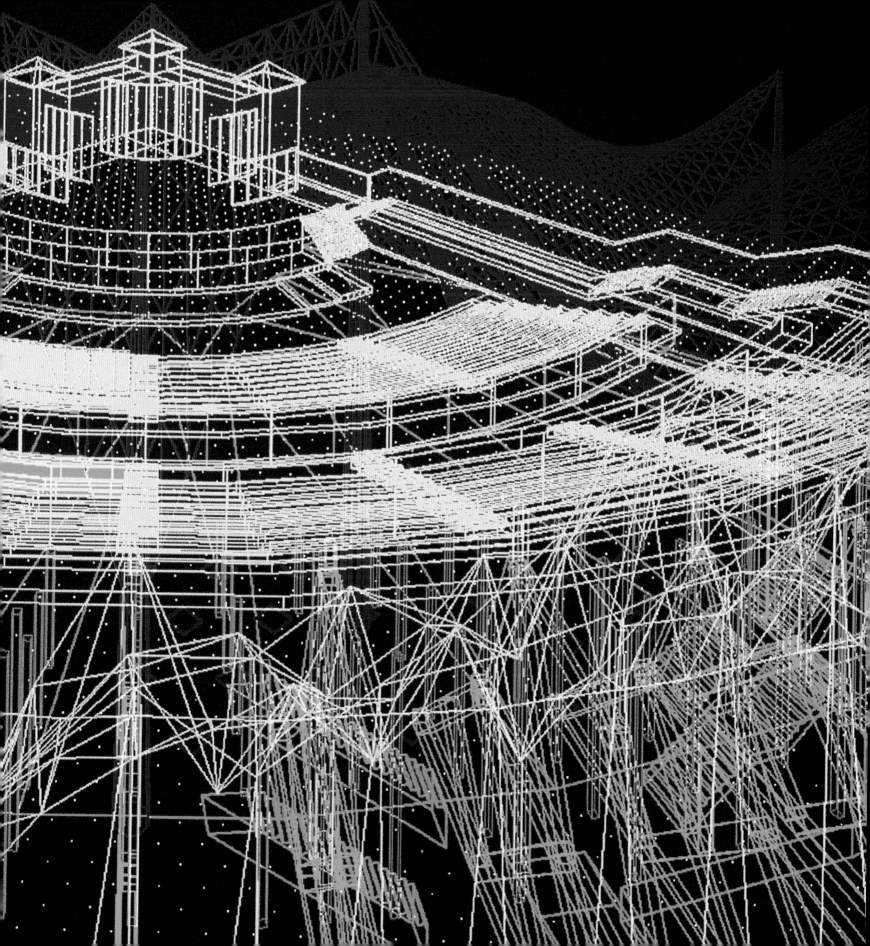

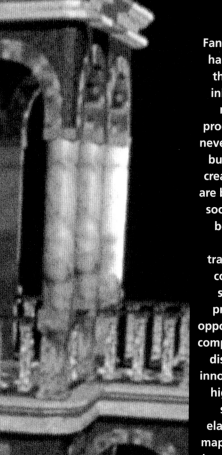

Fantasy architecture has been a part of the architectural inheritance, with many designs produced that were never intended to be built. The need to create projects that are beyond financial, social and political boundaries has today been transferred to the computer. Such schemes have provided useful opportunities for the computer scientist to display technical innovations, such as highly reflective surfaces and elaborate texture maps. Here are two imaginary interiors constructed by computer.

The computer is not just being applied to the design of buildings, but also to their interior organization. As large urban buildings become more complex, the clients' task becomes ever more difficult as they seek to maintain or improve the building. To do this efficiently, they need to know where everything is – from the telephones to the computers and the office furniture. Facility management is a considerable problem, so once the design is complete, a computer database can be used to monitor the building, not only in the physical sense, but also in terms of its environmental control and security. Inset, right: CAD software used for facilities management in a building.

The architectural facade is another area where the computer is consistently being used to explore design alternatives and to examine the impact of a particular proposal on the surrounding urban landscape. Above: exterior visualization from San Francisco – the building as sign. The use of floodlighting can now be simulated, so that clients can see how their building would look at night (right). Left: proposed scheme for a London Underground station, a complex modelling project. The computer can give the client a realistic impression of how the final scheme will look.

The intelligent building is another innovative idea, with its ability not only to monitor individual conditions – registering the amount of sunlight, for example, and adjusting the window blinds accordingly – but to oversee a series of individual computer-based systems. This avoids the increasingly tedious need, in the home, to program the video player, washing machine, dishwasher, hi-fi system and telephone answering machine as separate systems. It is not inconceivable that these appliances could negotiate amongst themselves, combining with people sensors to provide an editable background at both home and work.

In the third category, that of creative design, it is difficult, as yet, to see much evidence of software development. This is not surprising, as the emphasis so far has been on supporting routine and innovative design tasks. Until techniques of artificial intelligence really come of age, this category will not find many examples to support its existence.

Graphic Design

Of all the design professions, graphic design seems to have been most affected by the introduction of computer systems. Unlike architecture, it does not have a strong theoretical framework that could provide a perspective on the use of the new technology. The response has therefore tended to be pragmatic. Will the computer cause typography to degenerate? Will the fine edge of graphic creativity inevitably be blunted?

These are still current discussions in graphic design circles, particularly in Europe. The democratization of typography, made possible by the computer, is a shocking prospect for many designers, who see untrained users, armed with their computers and desktop-publishing software, successfully invading the very core of the profession.

However, the issues that concern the new wave of graphic designers are altogether different. Having understood the implications of the new technology, they are currently demonstrating what can be achieved within the electronic environment. They see the new technology as an exciting opportunity to look at things differently, and to examine what kinds of innovative design formulations are going to be appropriate in the future.

Graphic design is going to be not a print-based, but a hybrid activity, where the difference between previously separate domains is reduced; where existing design and production skills are merged into a digital equivalence; and where the need to acquire new skills is a continuing consequence of change.

These new skills involve understanding the importance of page description languages, such as 'Postscript'. Now a *de facto* standard for this type of communication, Postscript marks a milestone in the evolution of digital typography, as it links the laser printer to the computer in a close-coupled event. The description of fonts as mathematically scalable curves means that the designer is able to use a wide range of fonts in a variety of sizes. The computer will calculate what visual emphasis in thickness or curvature is necessary, thus removing some of the mystique surrounding type design.

From these developments have grown design ideas based on a layering principle, where image is laid upon image. These exploit a strong software function, and the resulting design has a virtual depth, because of the complexity of the overlays.

One of the most popular uses of the computer has been in graphic design. Entire double-page spreads can be designed on screen, with all the correct type styles and sizes together with black-and-white or colour illustrations. The final layouts can be colour-separated and the type sent to an image-setter – all from the designer's desk: a dramatic illustration of the way in which traditional skills have been compressed. Right: desktop-publishing layout.

One major reason for the increased popularity of desktop-publishing was the software package 'Postscript', which revolutionized the graphic design print industry and became a standard way of digitally describing a page. This software dealt with text and illustrations in a seamless electronic environment which changed the way designers thought about their work. Application software such as 'Pagemaker' and 'Quark Xpress', combined with lower prices in hardware, higher-

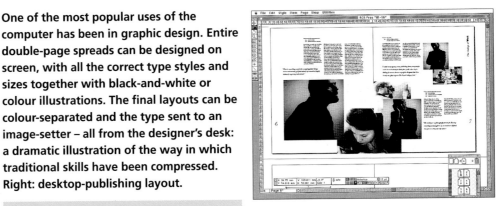

resolution computer screens and reliable hardcopy devices, set the scene for the computer to invade the traditional demarcations of graphic design.

The early application of the new technology to graphic design speeded up and enhanced existing working practices and areas of competency. However, younger practices have begun to look at the implications of the technology for imagery and to examine the potential of an entirely new creative language. Right: poster produced for *Design Quarterly*.

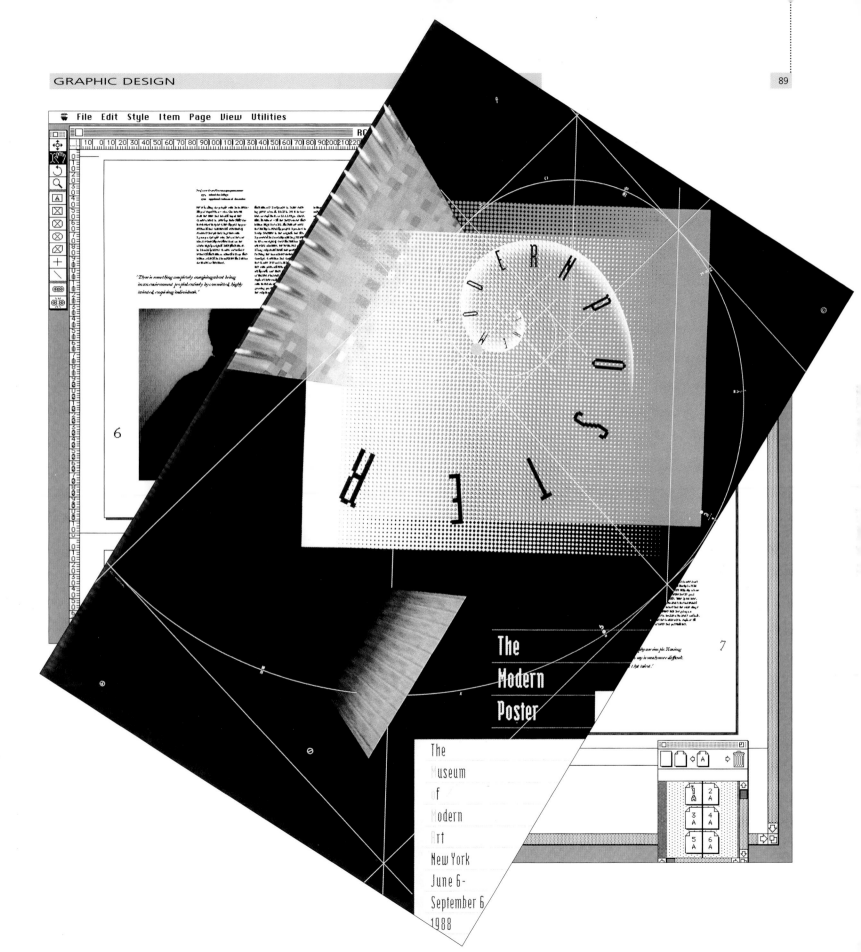

The
Modern
Poster

The
Museum
of
Modern
Art
New York
June 6–
September 6
1988

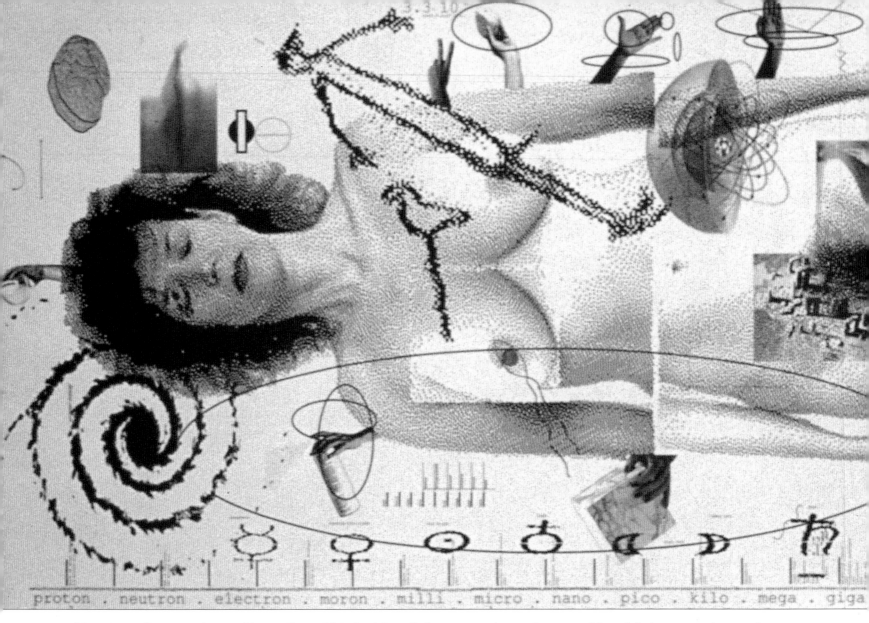

proton . neutron . electron . moron . milli . micro . nano . pico . kilo . mega . giga

This poster collage was designed by April Greiman for *Design Quarterly*, published by the Walker Art Museum, which devoted an entire issue to her work. Her idea was to make a poster that folded up into the back of the magazine, with a life-size collage image of herself on one side and examples of her work on the other. The poster shows how the layering of images can be used as a general compositional technique, as well as a means of providing details of intimate interest.These can be seen as offering more information, as they are examined in greater depth – a new kind of pluralism. For example, the bottom of the poster

(if, indeed, it really has a top or bottom) contains a technological timescale which spans from the birth of the solar system to the launch of the Macintosh computer in 1984. Other spaces are left blank, perhaps to take in other developments as they occur. In another corner there is a small-scale image of the entire poster with a simple statement that it contains 289,322 bytes of memory.

The entire poster was created on a Macintosh computer, with scanned and video images being worked on at the same time as the text. All the components were there to start with and allowed for

accidental design contortions as they were manipulated within the computer. Right: *Architecture: Education and Instruction*, another April Greiman poster collage for *Design Quarterly*.

Far right: the work on fabric for the Polyester Institute of Japan shows how designers are edging across the boundaries of their disciplines. Within a digital framework they are able to contemplate working in other areas with some measure of authority, demonstrating a fluid integration of their design skills.

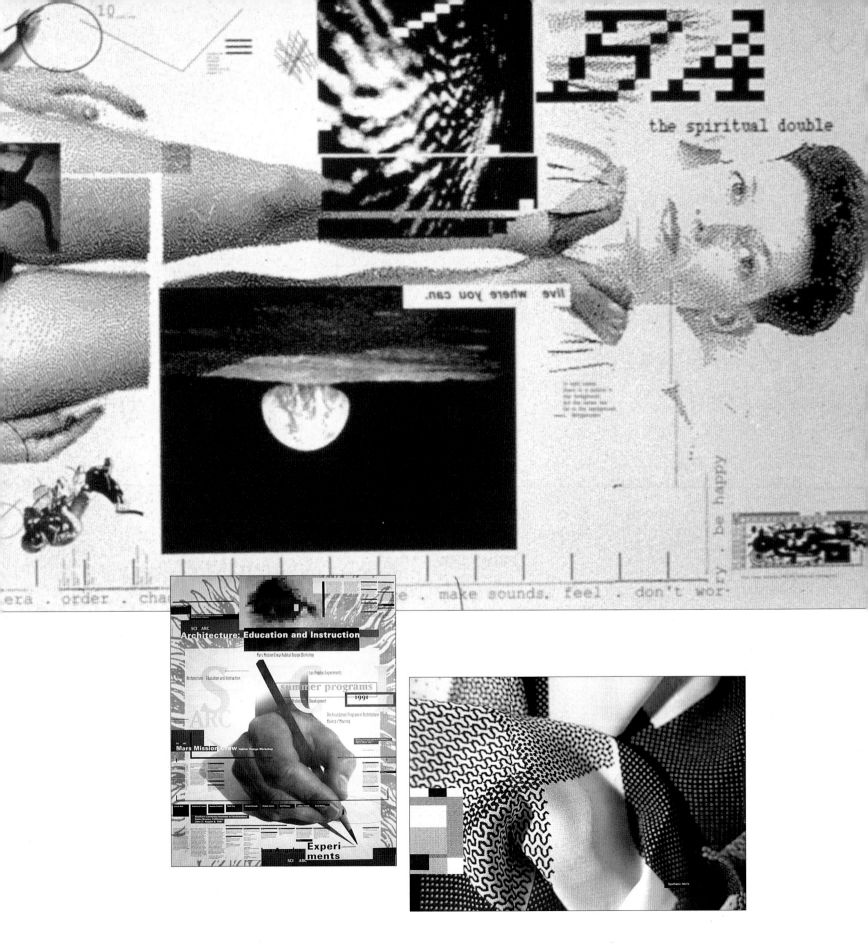

the spiritual double

live where you can.

be happy

era . order . cha...

... . make sounds . feel . don't wor...

SCI ARC

Architecture: Education and Instruction

Mars Mission Crew Habitat Design Workshop

Los Angeles Experiments

Architecture: Education and Instruction

summer programs

1991

The Foundation Program in Architecture

Making / Meaning

Mars Mission Crew Habitat Design Workshop

Experiments

SCI ARC

Many design agencies are developing their technological 'handwriting' as they seek to use computer systems in a creative way. Educational institutions have also begun to establish how documents of the future should look and feel. Above: exhibition poster for the Walker Art Museum (1989–90). Right: poster entitled '24-hour Turnaround' produced by Mark Anderson Design. Far right: 'An Exercise in Utilities' reproduced in *MacWorld* magazine .

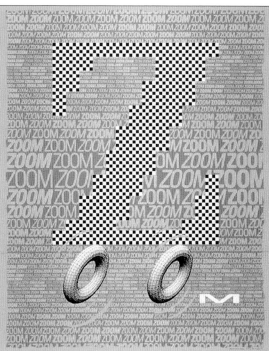

Left: poster for a computer-related design
course held at the Royal College of Art,
London. Below: textile design.
Bottom left: design for 'The New Discourse:
Cranbrook Design 1980–90'.

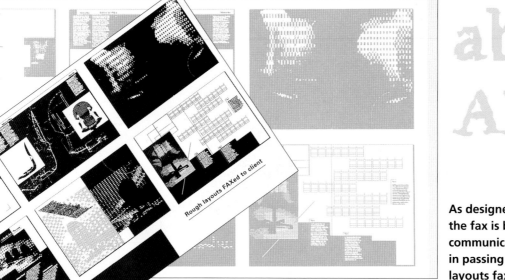

Rough layouts FAXed to client

As designers compress the iterative cycle, the fax is beginning to be recognized as a communication tool of the first importance in passing on design intentions. Left: rough layouts faxed to clients for approval.

The classic authority of legibility and of the type itself has been challenged by the new generation of computer-based designers. Their new skill base allows them to proclaim, in the words of typographic designer Rick Poynor: 'In the age of the desktop computer, font design software and page makeup programs, type has acquired a fluidity of physical outline, an ease of manipulation and, potentially, a lack of conceptual boundaries unimaginable only a few years ago.'[1] Max Kisman adds: 'Type is going to be as abstract as sand on the beach. In that sense type does not exist any more.'[2]

Another approach puts a random value into type software to make the result apparently more responsive, and certainly less predictable. This could be seen as entirely opposite to the rather tedious, clean and well-reproduced images that have so far been the objective of the computer software developpers, working at the behest of the design establishment.

It is not only type that is undergoing this revolution. Illustrations can now be decomposed into lines and tangents, or composed from bits of images taken from numerous sources. Collaging as a technique has been considerably extended by the use of computer systems, as it is simple to scan images, to cut and paste sections in a seamless manner, to manipulate them and then insert them into an overall design. The resulting visual complexity and high level of integration have seldom been equalled in the context of traditional media. Photographs, once the most reliable form of representation, have also been affected by the new computer skills. Changes can be made to the characteristics of an image in a more fundamental and convincing manner than has ever before been possible.

abcdefghijklmnopqrst
ABCDEFGHIJKLMNOPQR

abcdefghijklmnop
ABCDEFGHIJKLM

abcdefghijklmn
ABCDEFGHIJKL

Besides developing these new skills, which could be seen as extensions of traditional graphic design expertise, the new designer is going to have to cope with sound and moving images. Access to images will no longer be linear, with one event following another; the user of this new

Left: constructing type in the computer. It has been argued that desktop-publishing systems have made clear, well-produced type commonplace. So two Dutch designers have produced what have been termed 'random typefaces' (left). These distort according to how much 'randomness' is included by the designer. In other words, by varying the random factor in the computer, a slightly different type is produced each time. This means that type can alter as the weather changes, or gradually decay until it becomes unreadable.

medium will have multiple access, with a number of events happening in parallel. The new graphic designers (or whatever they come to be called) will need to have the skills to cope with such issues; they will need to link up with other areas of expertise, so that the design, rather than the discipline, dictates what can be done. San Francisco-based graphic designer Clement Mok declared in 1991: 'Instead of being type designers, photographers, and illustrators, we need to dabble skilfully in many realms. Graphic designers need to become good generalists and good collaborators – one of the strategic team of "invisible" professionals like, for example, a business or legal consultant.'[3] They will need to feel relaxed and comfortable with the non-print technology and with the new distribution media, such as CDI and CD-ROM (see p. 183).

Dumping Core No. 1, Medici Hinterwelt: Steve Pochin's work ably demonstrates the visual complexity of the computer collage, in which images are cut, pasted and distorted, so that the finished work demonstrates the very process of image creation. It does not represent the 'real', but constructs an image that is entirely self-referential and in constant flux, because the new digital tools are for changing, replacing and transforming, not for creating stasis.

Textile and Fashion Design

These areas of design were once closely geared to the seasons; each year designers were expected to produce four sets of designs that reflected seasonal changes. However, commercial pressures have begun to split the four seasonal classifications into many smaller sections, inspired by other specifications – often media-driven – intended to increase turnover. Pop stars, such as Madonna, and films, such as *Out of Africa*, have influenced the designs of many fashion houses. The fashion industry – designers included – has had to accelerate its response by reducing design and production time. Today it is not unusual for a designer to produce between eight and ten collections per year, containing either completely new designs or variations on existing garments. Computerization has enabled this increase in turnover to be achieved without additional cost. Or perhaps it was the computer itself that engendered the multi-season year.

In any case, computerization of the fashion industry began at the production end, as this was the stage that was most amenable to digital conversion. Much effort was

In fashion design, software development has largely focused on areas that are readily applicable to computing, such as block work and pattern-making. The ease with which pattern blocks (opposite, above right) can be manipulated within the computer for the efficient grading and nesting of patterns (below left) made this aspect an obvious candidate for computerization.

Most first-generation software players in the industry made design claims for their systems, even though they were really production tools. And although Gerber and the French company Lectra, for example, later introduced computer paint systems to answer the needs of designers, it was still not possible to transfer information from the design end directly to production. Below: the Gerber system in action.

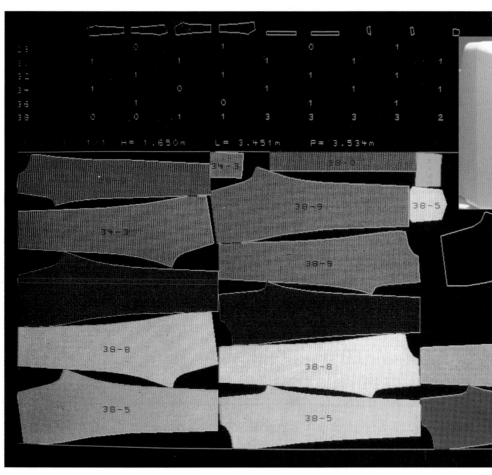

One exception to the dominance of production-biased systems was offered by Computer Design Inc. (CDI), who have developed software for fashion design since the early 1980s. Their system (opposite, above left, and below left and right) has been used by major fashion producers in Europe, the US and the Pacific Rim. Each software module deals with a separate aspect of production. It is possible to dye and spin a yarn, weave it into a cloth, and then design a garment by draping it over a three-dimensional model of a human figure or texture-wrapping it over a scanned photograph.

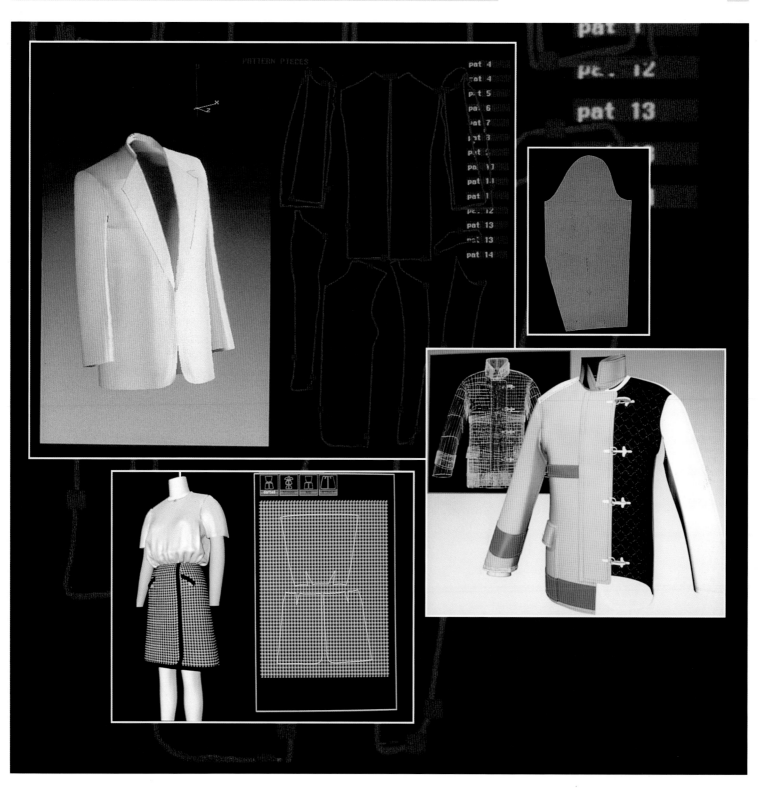

PATTERN PIECES

pat 4
pat 4
pat 5
pat 6
pat 7
pat 3
pat 9
pat 11
pat 11
pat 1
pat 12
pat 13
pat 13
pat 14

invested in developing computer tools to make the production of garments much more effective, but there was no link with the initial design process. The basis of the transformation from manual to electronic methods was the basic pattern block. Common to all garment design, it allows design variations to be developed from a given standard outline. As this process is conceptually very similar to the way in which computers handle information, many computer analysts saw the advantage of adapting their software to deal with problems of garment production. They tended to start by digitizing pattern blocks, which could then be optimally arranged to use least material, and either plotted onto paper or cut directly from cloth. This process became the basis of most of the computer systems used in the fashion industry.

Some computer software analysts saw an additional advantage in using three-dimensional models of the human figure, on which design iterations of the garment could be 'hung'. Once the designer considered the garment to be finished, it could then be 'unwrapped' to form two-dimensional patterns. This was conceptually a significant move forward, linking the design process directly to that of manufacture. However, few fashion companies were ready to take on the radical change in working methods implied by three-dimensional modelling techniques.

The move to computers in the fashion industry was not confined to the production process. They also began to appear in retail outlets for tracking customer preferences. Fashion retailers extended computerization to an electronic point of sale (EPOS). This provides direct information about buying habits, which is fed back to the stock warehouses and then on to the manufacturer. The result is a tight iterative circle of information feedback. It enables the design and production teams to determine what is happening, almost on a day-to-day basis, in the retail shops, and to follow it up with an immediate product response. Such a sensitive and rapid response mechanism would not be possible without the electronic channels provided by the computer. It has allowed

Above and right: texture-wrapped images created with the CDI fashion/textile computer system. By telescoping the design process, the CDI software challenges many of the boundaries that exist between textile and fashion designers and their technical support staff. It represents the fusing of fashion and textile design because it allows the designer to move between them, acting sometimes as a fashion designer and at other times as a textile creator. Once again, this increases the area of competency of the designer.

A research project of the Royal College of Art, London, conducted in association with major garment manufacturers in the United Kingdom, investigated how the new computational tools could aid the designer. The project used a conceptual framework borrowed from cognitive science, and employed computer animation skills to simulate the production of a garment. This provided appropriate information for a range of contributors, who form the design, production and marketing teams.

some companies a distinct advantage; within the very competitive fashion industry, the more information an organization has about its products, the more successful it can be in spotting and reacting to trends at the retail level.

There have been many recent attempts to consider how different methods of representation within the computer can be applied to specific design disciplines. Fashion/textile design is one area that has met with some success. Traditional forms of representation have been given new 'electronic' meanings and combined with computer animation techniques, with aspects of computer graphics and cognitive science, to provide new computer support tools for the fashion industry. This new generation of computational tools will replace the current, production-based tools, which represent little more than the electronic mechanization of essentially manual tasks.

Computer systems to serve the needs of the textile designer have developed in parallel with those for fashion designers. Because these design disciplines are very close, and have a large area of practical overlap, the introduction of computer systems consolidated the amalgamation of the two areas. However, the specific concerns of the textile designer, in terms of weave and knit, were initially dictated, as in the case of fashion design, by production needs. To an extent this isolated the designer, because the equipment, designed for large production runs, was inflexible, and consequently restricted the design input. It was not until the introduction of smaller, micro-based systems that the designer was able to reassert control over the process. The personal-computer-based software now found in many medium-sized design organizations allows considerable scope for design work and small-scale production, which is ideal for making sample garments.

The use of computers for the production of printed textiles was largely based on computerized paint systems, and it was some time before software appeared that was developed specifically for the textile designer. For the designer to meet demands for better quality, increased variety and opportunities for styling, computer-aided design systems had to improve their level of sophistication. They needed to meet these demands without constraining the design. This has happened, and textile designers now use computers to produce multiple colourways, pattern repeats and colour separations.

The work of the textile designer has been enhanced by the computer. Malcom Cox's approach, for example, moves away from an emphasis on production and towards design. Using software based on a paint system, he manages the entire process of design through to manufacture, printing on both paper and cloth.

Photography

The history of the development of photography has been likened to that of computing; both started life as new technologies that were able, through technological processes, to represent reality in a new way. Photography used the simple mechanism of the camera, while computing had to rely on the complex mechanism of the digital electronic computer.

In its early days, photography was perceived as a threat to painting because of its superior ability to display naturalistic images in fine detail and texture, with a minimum of skill on the part of the operator. This development coincided with the rise of the need for 'factual' information in the late nineteenth century, as science tried to describe the world as a series of discrete elements that could be captured and recorded. The ability of photography to provide an apparently accurate, precise documentary record of an event placed it in a commanding role. Thus, the photograph has come to hold a very special position, because it has a veracity that neither drawing nor painting share. It has become the medium by which things that have actually happened are set down on paper, and it reinforces our cultural preoccupation with the old adage 'seeing is believing'.

The development of the computer, with its ability to provide a seamless environment for retouching, has emasculated this aspect of photography, weakening its position as the prime, reliable recorder of reality. Commercially, this can be seen as a distinct advantage, as images recorded either on standard photographic film or using a video still camera can be transferred directly into the computer, and the image displayed on the computer monitor. It is then possible to manipulate the image, and the work of retouching can involve anything from the removal of small blemishes in the original photograph, to a complete colour change. It is possible to 'collage' many separate photographs to form a composite image. In the digital environment the photograph becomes completely editable, and therefore no longer necessarily represents what the camera originally saw.

During the past few years, electronic retouching and collaging has become an important development in the area of art direction. It has grown because of the acceptance of computers as part of the working environment of the advertising agencies and reproduction houses.

In artistic terms, this revaluation of photography has been championed by artists such as David Hockney, who in 1990 said 'We had this belief in photography, but that is about to disappear because of the computer. It can recreate something that looks like the photographs we've known. But it's unreal. What's that going to do to all photographs? It's going to make people say: that's just another invention. And I can see there's a side of it that's disturbing for us all. It's like the ground being pulled from underneath us.'[4]

This post-photographic age sees the computer in its role as a universal machine, capable of synthesizing traditional media and integrating them into a new, generalized image technology.

This kind of work represents high-resolution (print quality), digital image-processing. This is the top end of the huge electronic chain that starts with the camera and finishes with the printed magazine. Most of the steps between origination and production represent separate skills, but these have now begun to merge with the production process, which may start at the same time as the design. The Malvern Star Australian bicycle advertisement far left was constructed with the Quantel Paintbox, while the Crosfields Electronics Mamba system was used for the BMW advertisement 'No Way', by Mike Valente (left).

n bicycle.

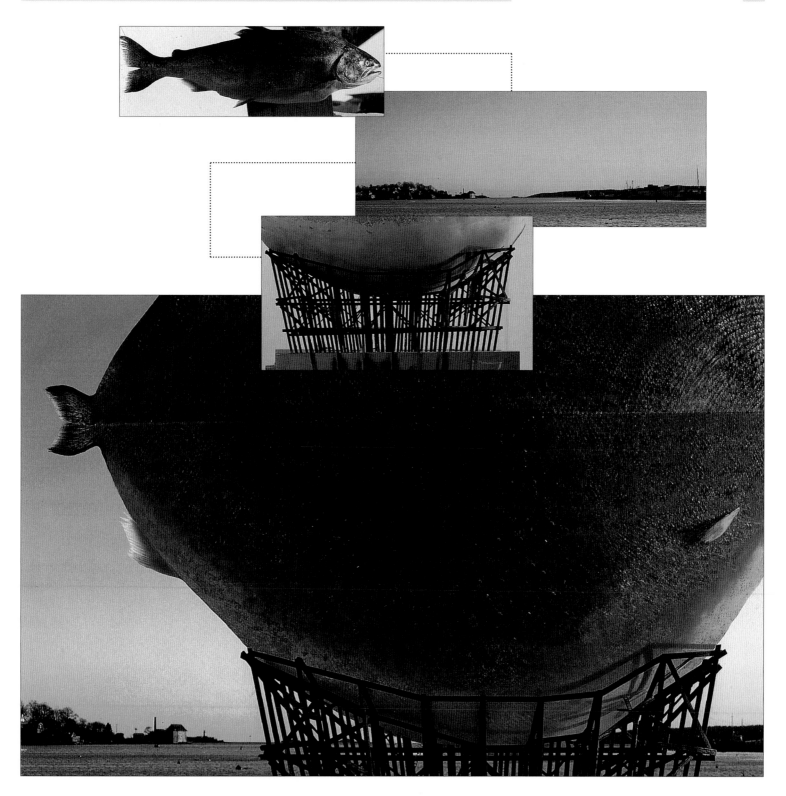

The Barco Graphics project for a Morey's Fish commercial shows how three separate shots can be combined electronically and then manipulated to obtain the desired emphasis. This result is produced at a resolution that competes very well with traditional photographic processes. Right: this fish image by Paul Biddle, created with the Crosfields Mamba system, has been electronically retouched.

These Montmartre Visuals show how a digital photographic set was created by seamlessly combining location shots of Paris with studio images of people. The idea was to model the image within the computer, rather than building an expensive and time-consuming full-size set. A model-maker produced a mock-up, about 50 cm high, of an appropriate building, and the people were photographed separately. The whole thing was then put together using a Barco Graphics computer.

David Hockney first explored the border area between painting and photography using the traditional photographic techniques of the Polaroid camera. The development of the video still camera has provided artists with a more innovative tool, because it challenges so many conventions of the photographer's craft. With the video still camera, items such as colour-correction lenses are no longer necessary, and f-stops are redundant, as all such adjustments can be made with the aid of a computer after the photograph has been taken. Colour has always been important in the work of Hockney, and decisions about its use have until now had to be made in direct relation to painting. Now it is possible to consider colour as an element that is editable at any stage in the creative process. Colour has been separated from the medium of expression. Here we see two video still composite portraits produced by Hockney in 1990: left, Colin Ford, and right, Lisa McPherson.

Design Crafts

The use of computer systems in areas of design such as architecture, engineering, industrial design and graphic design is now well established. But there are other areas of design, notably the crafts, where it has yet to have a major impact on the way objects are designed and made. There may be very good reasons why crafts such as ceramics or jewelry have been left largely intact in the march toward computerization.

From a practical standpoint, the cost of computer systems has been prohibitive for all but large companies, who are able to write off their technological investments against extensive projects or large-volume production runs. The crafts, by contrast, have been largely under-capitalized. The software available for design tends to be production-orientated, and is therefore mainly useful only after designers have made up their minds on the form of the product, and when it is ready for manufacture. In the crafts, production issues tend to be of lesser importance. Malleable materials are often used very interactively to produce visually complex objects, frequently designed and made on a very small scale by individuals.

Theoretical considerations may also have constrained attempts to introduce computing into the crafts. Manual processes require many years of practice before it is possible to produce objects that represent a full flowering of the craftsperson's talent. Traditional training for ceramicists and jewelers often covers an entire career. But the introduction of computing could, by implication, shortcircuit years of dutiful application to a craft by building the resident skills into the software. This may be perceived as an unacceptable threat, for when skills are built in, artistic consent is often 'built out'. The concern of the craftsperson is that, if this skill transference does take place, professional control over design decisions would diminish.

But circumstances and attitudes are changing. The new generation of designer-craftspersons is looking to technology to increase their design expertise, so closing the gap between the design idea and its practical realization. This involves moving towards an engineering approach to issues such as visualization and production. The traditional hand/eye feedback of the craftsperson will probably be superseded by the more controlled, but less tactile, computer approach. Perhaps this is best expressed as a transference of skill, rather than its replacement.

The craft industries still tend primarily to be very small and labour-intensive, employing only a few designer-makers. There are some large companies, however, which dominate manufacturing and the marketplace through linked retail outlets. Both types of organization are fashion-driven and need to be flexible enough to respond quickly to market trends. The smaller companies benefit from their limited size, which allows them to produce experimental work with relative ease. The larger organizations rely on computer technology to make them more responsive in a market that is becoming increasingly competitive.

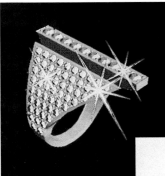

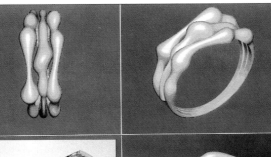

The nature of the craft industries has meant an intermittent start to the introduction of technology. Stewart Devlin is just one practitioner who has designed a range of jewelry and furniture. He uses three-dimensional modelling software that creates rendered screen images and provides details on the weight of the object – a crucial consideration in the pricing of jewelry. It is important to be able to scale a design up or down, maintaining the specific relationships of the various parts. Precision drilling in such small objects can also save considerable time in the final production phase. Devlin's computer system has enabled him to reduce the design and approval cycle from the original six weeks to a matter of days. These images were created with an Intergraph system. The ring design is seen both as a screen image (above left) and as a finished product. Above right: three views of a second ring design by Devlin. These enable the designer to check how the finished product will look from different angles.

A rather different style of jewelry design is represented by the work of Tony Pack. The frame-grabbed image of a woman (below) shows how the piece will look when worn.

The stereolithography process (below) opens up new manufacturing possibilities for a range of jewelry.

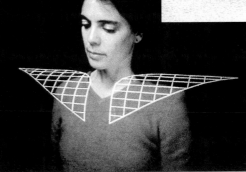

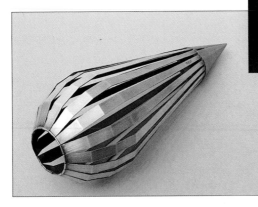

Young designer Rebecca de Quin used two-dimensional drawing software to provide a template for cutting the silver sheet to make this pomander (left). It is an ideal tool, as it is less wasteful than conventional methods and allows for accurate detailing on complex shapes.

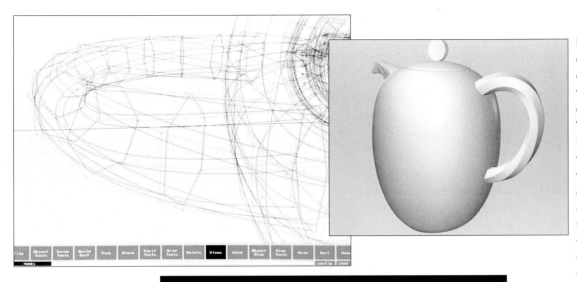

In ceramics much design-led computer work tends to focus on surface decoration, though there are some cases of experimentation with form. The early examples shown below left demonstrate how texture-wrapping could simulate the effect of various glazes and decorative effects. Alias three-dimensional modelling software was used by David Queensbury to evaluate the design proposal for a ceramic coffee pot (left and far left).

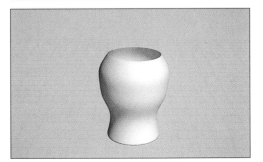

Applying human judgment to expert systems is a difficult area, and in the context of the computer such issues become very complex indeed. The software package 'Knowledge from Beauty', developed in Chicago, generates ceramic forms at random (right, above and below), and asks users to express their preferences. The computer then 'learns' about their particular tastes, and continues to develop forms within the agreed constraints, asking the user to vote 'yes' or 'no' in response to each form.

Film and Animation

The cinema has not remained immune to the influence of the new technologies, but it has had a surprisingly chequered response, considering that the moving picture is itself a relatively recent and purely technological phenomenon.

The image of the computer held great interest for the film industry, and early attempts to give that image some substance produced a stylistic impression of what the technology looked like, or, more accurately, of how film-directors -- and audiences -- expected a computer to look and behave. At this very early stage in development, the visual image of computer graphics was way beyond its practical realization, and had to be synthesized with traditional techniques.

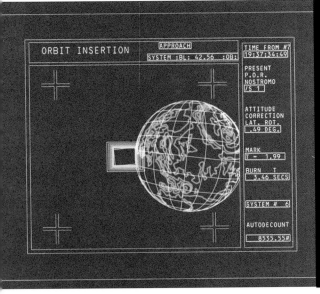

It is difficult to establish just where and when the first computer-generated sequence was used in a film. *Alien* **was certainly among the first to use computer-generated images within the main body of the film, as opposed to the title sequence. The computer graphics were restricted to computer screens, so most of the displays were textual; information was typed in on a keyboard, and the computer appeared to answer. The only computer-generated image was a wireframe contour map of the surface of a planet on which the spaceship was going to land (left).**

Tron, produced by Walt Disney in 198?, was the first film to attempt to demonstrate the full range of visually creative effects that could be produced by computer. It concerns a computer programmer who attempts to prove his suspicions about the honesty of his boss by entering the computer system itself. The idea of the film was to combine the latest computer techniques with backlit animation to create a seamless production with the look and feel of a computer arcade game. The traditional technique was very simple; the actors' white costumes were covered with patterns of black lines, representing computer circuits, and photographed against a black backdrop. Each frame of the film was then photographically enlarged as a black and white transparency, backlit to make the figures glow, and finally rephotographed.

It is interesting to discover how limited computer-generated work was in the early 1980s. Much simulated computer graphics had to be introduced, using traditional methods, to match expectations of the visual quality of computer graphics. This synthetic approach provided a convenient hook on which to hang an image of the future, particularly in science-fiction films.

In the cinema, as in many other areas of design, there was little understanding of how the scope of the computer could be broadened – beyond its use as an image of hi-tech. Film-makers used the computer purely for generating the kind of work that they knew and understood. The perceived high cost of computer-generated work meant that few directors were willing to take the risk of using such untried technology in an innovative way.

This was soon to change, and by the late 1980s there was growing confidence that technological advances in hardware and software could yield an entirely new product at

Companies such as Pixar and Symbolics began to produce high-quality computer animation shorts demonstrating what could be done with the new technology – though without trying to find any new form of expression. The animations were almost indistinguishable from those produced using traditional techniques. *Tin Toy* won an Oscar for animation, and *Stanley and Stella* made Symbolics a central player in the animation industry. Left: a snowman animation by Pixar.

a competitive price. Computer techniques now looked far less as though they were machine-generated, and, combined with emerging talent amongst designers, this encouraged the growth of computer character animation, as distinct from computer graphics. The technical task of constructing images of the human body to create imaginary people has been the major goal of many computer graphics companies for the last decade.

Such techniques introduced a new concept of computer-generated film, by moving from the computer animation of imaginary people to the digital re-creation of dead actors, performing against a digital background. Early attempts had many faults; the characters lacked personality, and the movements were stiff and unconvincing. But they demonstrated that a synthetic production was technically feasible. If certain aspects of artificial intelligence could be incorporated, it would be possible to achieve not only the goal of visual realism, but that of behavioural realism too. This opens up enormously creative possibilities for producing digital illusions. An interactive film, using synthetic actors working within an entirely synthetic set, could be produced with a thousand different endings, for example. The consequences are, however, potentially unnerving. Dead actors could be re-created and made to perform roles they had never played in real life, in conjunction with living actors.

While this theoretical work was progressing in various research laboratories and software houses, the commercial studios of Hollywood were using more and more computer-generated work. A series of science-fiction films, the work of some perceptive directors, such as George Lucas and Ridley Scott, began to show what could be done with computer-generated techniques within the framework of the popular cinema. But few serious attempts have been made to create a full-length, computer-generated film, and they probably never will be made within the commercial cinema. The development of special effects techniques – often called 'impact aesthetics' – is the current preoccupation, as each film tries to outdo the previous production by generating increasingly elaborate techniques to impress an ever-expectant audience.

It is now commonly accepted that many technologies are in the process of merging. It is impossible to talk about the cinema, virtual reality, television or the recent development of High-Definition Television (HDTV) as though they were separate, isolated technologies. The future of film cannot therefore be considered without taking account of these technologies.

Many feel that high-definition television, with its ability to provide pictures of a much higher resolution, displayed on a wider screen, with improved colour and sound quality, is the natural successor to current television. Others consider that television should follow the direction opened up by the computer. This would result in a form of television that would offer the viewer real choice. Television as a service, they feel, would benefit from its capacity to carry other forms of information.

Virtual reality (see p. 149) is potentially the most immersive and interactive of the emergent technologies, and it could represent a major new direction for the cinema, enabling us to move beyond synthetic films to some form of all-encompassing spatial environment. The members of the audience, now the active participators, no longer look through a two-dimensional window; they become part of the film itself. Perhaps the film of the twenty-first century will provide sensory feedback, wide field-of-view screens, and wearable interactive devices, which will demolish the current boundaries of the third-party observer.

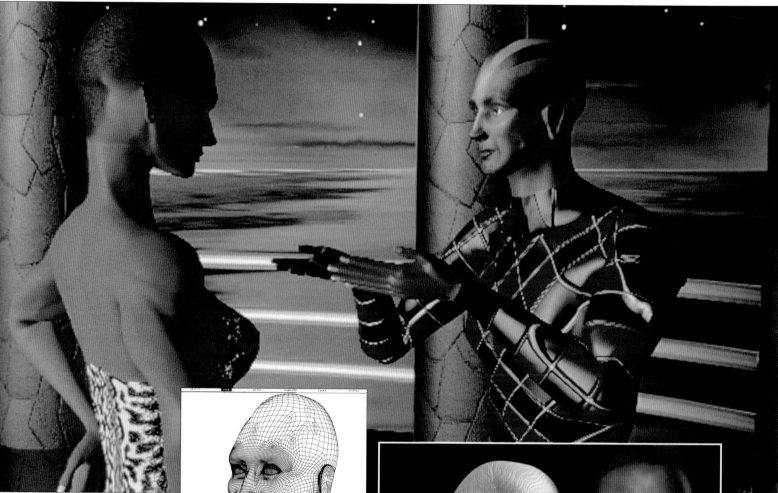

The computer company Symbolics produced a series of computer animations based on their 1989 star Lotta Desire. This leopardskin-clad woman plays a major role in a short piece of animation called *Virtually Yours*. It shows the beautiful Lotta waiting for her lover, who takes so long to arrive that she becomes an old woman – still recognizable, but with a rather sad expression. Matt Elson, the designer, spent considerable time developing synthetic characters, and the increasing realism of these films demonstrates how he is moving closer to his goal of being unable to distinguish a virtual actor from a real one.

In the 1989 film *The Abyss* (below and insets below left) the decision to go ahead with investing in the new technology was fully justified, as the 'pseudopod' became one of the most highly proclaimed computer images of the late 1980s. The pod is a thin finger of water that penetrates an oil rig. When it meets some of the crew, the end of the water finger reflects the human faces that it 'sees'. It took six months of intensive work to produce a convincing and realistic form for the pod, which became a fully animated object, reflecting the interior of the rig.

The astonishing ability of the computer to transform one image into another that is totally different is revealed here through a series of discrete steps (below to right).

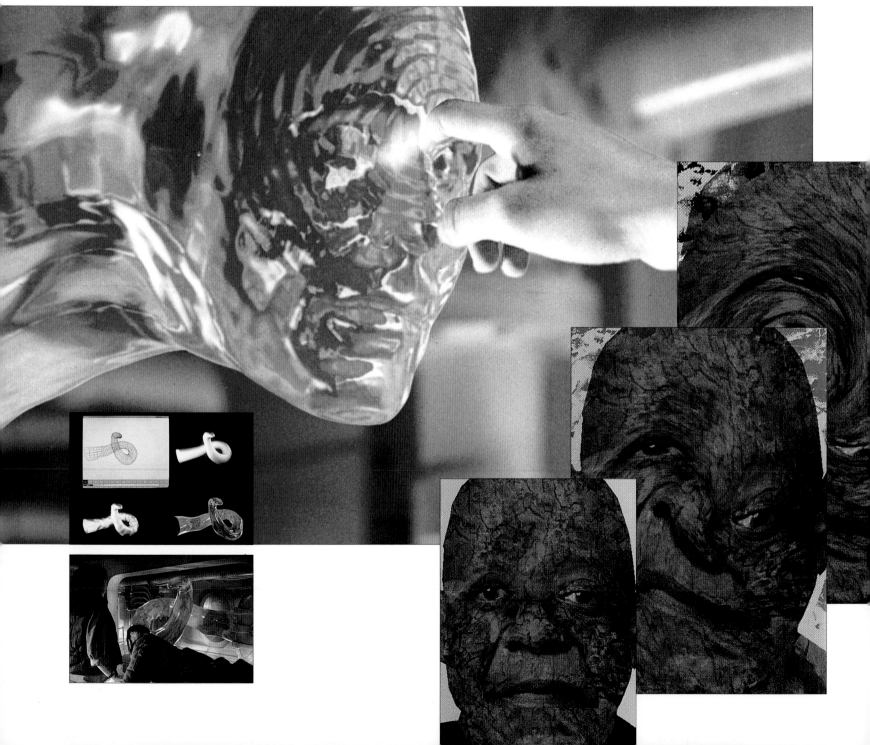

The intelligent characterization of the human form in the computer is being worked on by Daniel Thalmann and Nadia Magnenat-Thalmann. They are beginning to produce a realistic computer representation of human behaviour. There could soon exist an almost independent character, perhaps able to learn from situations and respond to others in a way that is virtually indistinguishable from 'real' actors. *Rendez-vous à Montréal*, for example, is a seven-minute, computer-generated film that attempts to recreate Marilyn Monroe as synthetic character.

Above: stills from the Thalmann films *Flashback* (above left) and *Still Walking* (above right).

Computer animation has been used for some time within a conventional framework, but recent developments have provided alternative methods. Live action can be created by using a Cyber-glove and flying mouse, which animate the characters as virtual puppets. Mr Film of California has designed *Silver Suzy* (right) to create performance animation, driven by real actors in a way similar to that in which puppeteers control puppets.

The Lawnmower Man (1992) used extensive computer graphics techniques, including the now famous 'Cybersex' scene. Loosely based on a Stephen King short story, the film traces the transition between the

real world and virtual reality. Above: in this scene the central character, CyberJoe, disembodies an antagonist. A 'particulation' effect is used to turn the character into random particles, which vibrate away from each other.

Right: in ILM's film *Terminator 2: Judgment Day,* the challenge was to create a convincing character who would blend into the live action in a seamless manner, as no scene in the movie was completely computer-generated. ILM produced a very successful characterization for T-1000, the humanoid, who moves backwards and forwards between his true form as a silvery metal robot and his incarnation as an American police officer.

Painting

The art of the late nineteenth and twentieth centuries can be characterized as a struggle to come to terms with technological developments, represented first by the emergence of photography, then of film and television, and finally of the computer. These inventions have changed the way in which artists have both approached and constructed their work. The new technologies – in particular photography, film and visual computing – have in turn looked to painting to provide a cultural framework for their development; they wanted to be accepted as part of the spectrum of artistic, rather than scientific achievement.

In the nineteenth century, photography was at first characterized as a rival to art, but it later became accepted as an art form in its own right. Film challenged both the novel, in storytelling, and art, in representing the moving image, and soon established a theoretical basis that firmly linked it with the arts. Early computer image-makers also saw themselves as artists, or at least as bridging the gap between art and science, and constructed often ill-famed attempts at computer art. Probably no other period has had to deal with so many conflicting demands. Never before have so many new techniques and activities pressurized the fine arts, vying for inclusion in the aesthetic canon. Never before have we been asked to make so great an adjustment to the boundary of what is considered 'art'.

Early experiments in the application of computing to the whole range of the arts provided the impetus to develop software to make music, write poetry and create dance. The computer's contribution to musical production has been significant, particularly in France and the USA. But the predominant use of computing in the sphere of the arts has been the creation of the visual image.

As we saw in Chapter One (p. 24), painting within computer systems has taken two, often opposing, paths. The first simply uses the computer as a tool to produce 'paintings' in the traditional sense. The development of the ubiquitous computer paint system has provided the software for this activity (see p. 41). Painting software is now moving into the third generation with sophisticated general-purpose techniques, such as animation. These begin to exploit the unique capabilities of the computer, moving further away from the original painting metaphor, towards a vision of the computer as an active partner rather than a passive toolbox.

Computer modelling systems have also been used by artists to simulate work in the traditional three-dimensional context. These artists produce their work using the tools of the engineer, designer and architect – the three-dimensional modelling computer systems that were conceived to construct aircraft, cars and buildings – unrestrained by the need to manufacture. They construct images that are neither painting nor sculpture, but exist somewhere between the two-dimensional and the three-dimensional, in an area of overlap that traditional media have been unable to explore. Computer journalist Barbara

An early development in computer graphics was the computer paint system. It enabled marks to be made on the screen that looked increasingly like those produced by traditional painting materials. Remarkable electronic paintings have been produced, some indistinguishable from 'real' paintings. Others retain the look and feel of computer-generated artwork. Left: *The Circus Animals' Desertion*.

Robertson describes the process vividly: 'When I was painting, the canvas became a wall I couldn't get through, now I can pass beyond the picture plane. I can move around three-dimensional objects inside a three-dimensional space. It's like sculpture, except I cannot touch, and unlike sculpture I can cross exterior boundaries and go inside.'[5]

The second path that computer artists have taken looks at what the software can do when it is given greater autonomy. Their work depends on a rule-based computer system, combined with techniques from artificial intelligence. The outcome challenges our perceptions of what constitutes art, and where the art resides. Does it lie within the drawing or painting that has been produced, within the software, or within the artist's imagination?

If there was an intellectual difficulty in using paint systems to produce paintings, then the idea that the machine could become autonomous and create images in its own right is even more unacceptable to most artists. Such a position is extreme and confronts the entire basis of western art, which has always assumed that the creative act is in some way connected with human intervention. This therefore marks an entirely new departure for artistic endeavour. It is set to demonstrate a new phase in the – until now – difficult relationship between art and technology.

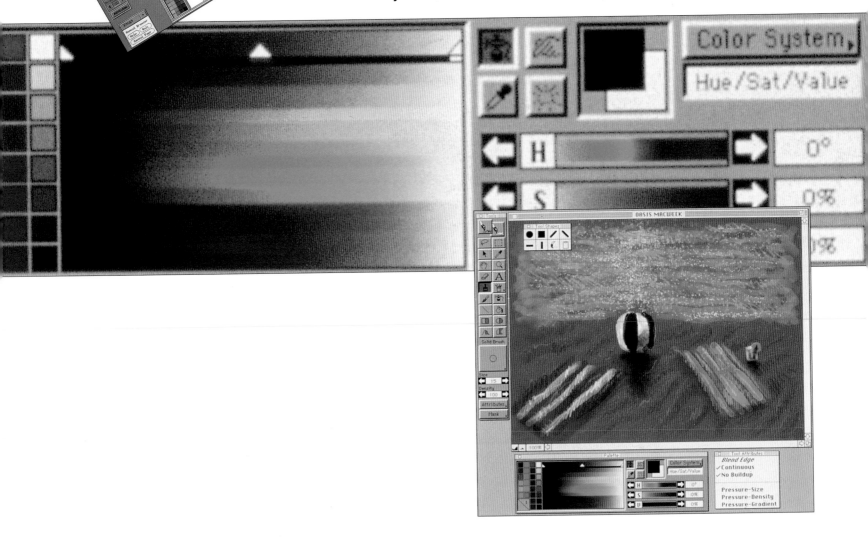

The third generation of paint software strives to imitate many traditional media, such as watercolour, pencil, crayon and pastel. Left and below: software palettes.

In certain systems that emulate watercolour, the artist can start with slightly damp 'paper', and then use the computer 'brush' to apply varying amounts of 'water and paint'. The 'dry brush' effect closely resembles the scratchy marks a dry brush leaves on paper. Alternatively, areas can be blurred, as though with a wet sponge, to create softer outlines. Opposite, above and below: watercolour techniques in play. Opposite, centre left: gouache technique.

Pressure sensitivity is an important recent development for the electronic brush and pencil. As more pressure is applied to the brush, a wider mark is made, and when pressure is applied to the pencil, the line and colour become more distinct. In addition, these packages allow the artist to 'cut out' parts of the drawing and 'paste' them on to other areas. Commands such as 'merge' mean that different parts of the work can be joined, while 'transparency' allows the freedom to overlay colour; 'erase' will remove an area as completely as if it had never existed.

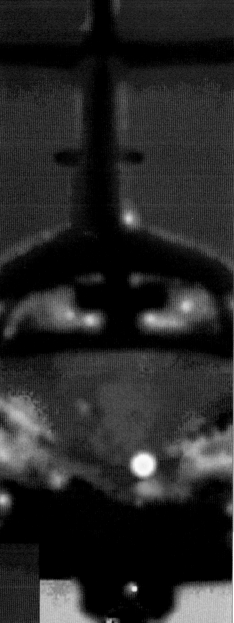

Artists have also experimented with three-dimensional modelling, adapting software that was primarily designed for other functions. The resulting images sometimes have the feel of the three-dimensional models produced on engineering CAD systems, with the artist striving to make the image work as an aesthetic statement. Some, however, heavily exploit texture and lighting effects, extracting a particular shot from a sinuous, three-dimensional rendered environment. The work of Char Davies offers fine examples of this technique.

SOFTIMAGE

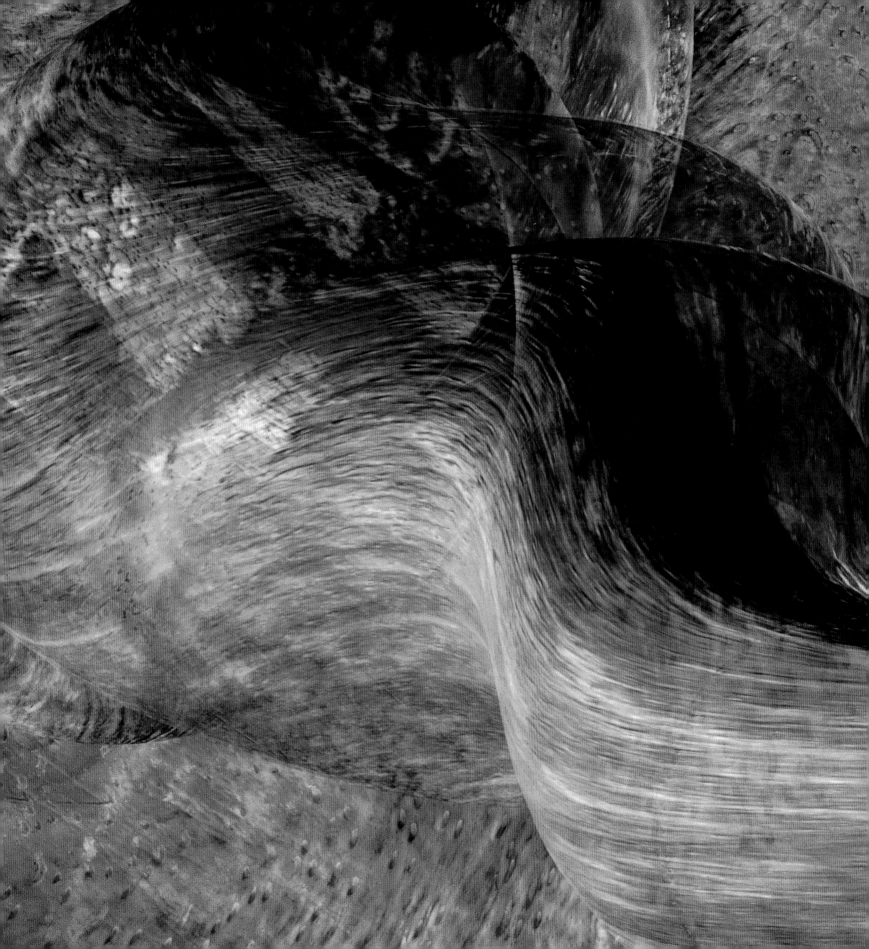

Printmakers have also recognized the advantages of using the computer for image generation. Max Davies has shown how a line illustration developed on the computer (right) can be translated via a silkscreen onto metal, and etched to create filigree work.

An alternative form of computer art uses programming to develop images. The work of Harold Cohen stands out in this context, representing an alternative to the argument that the software determines the art outcome. In other words, an image need not be put into a computer in order to get one out. Harold Cohen has programmed a computer to make drawings without any human intervention. The machine is able to produce quite naturalistic drawings entirely on its own. Built into the program is a set of rules, which to some extent govern the outcome of the image. They are like the rules in a game of chess in that, although each game is controlled by the basic rules, they are sufficiently flexible that they can lead to many different games. The difference is that in a game of chess, the player interprets the rules; in the work of Harold Cohen, it is the computer that interprets them.

The later drawings shown above are much more naturalistic than those of Cohen's earlier period. They take on many conventions of western art, with distance being suggested by the overlapping of objects. Perspective is also used in the conventional way to enhance the impression of distance. Some feel that these later images are not as evocative as the earlier drawings, because realism has, to a degree, got between the artist and the computer. They are more like conventional drawings, and could be mistaken for such. Above left: image from the *Eden* series. Above right: *Imagined Paradise*.

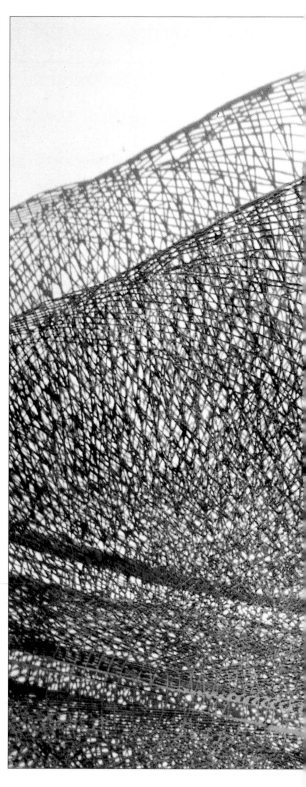

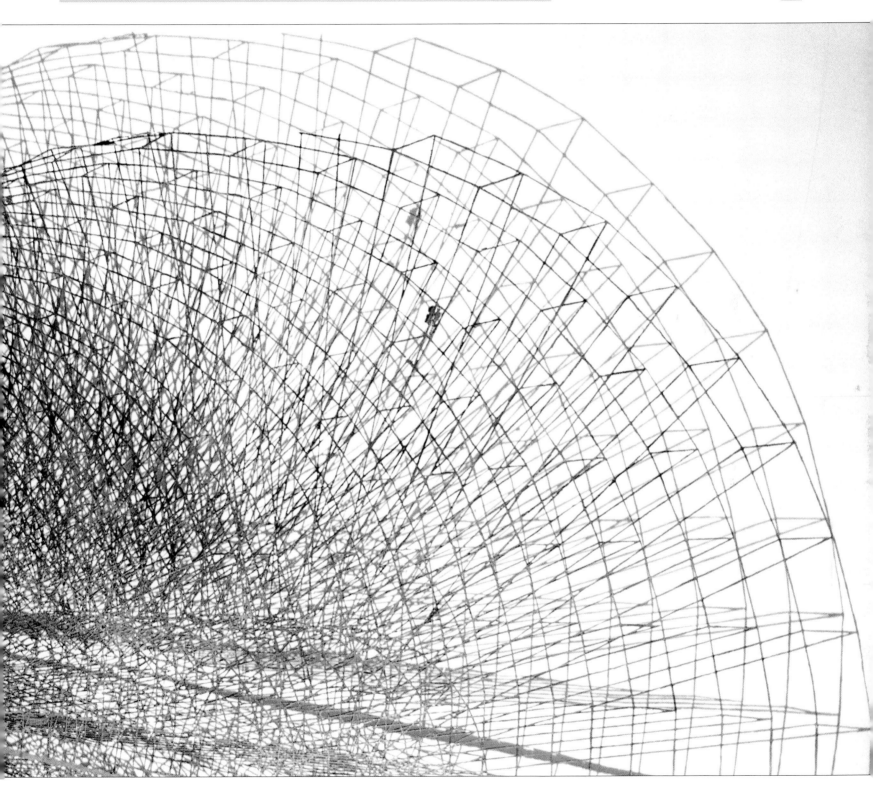

Kenneth Snelson is an American artist whose work explores the boundary between virtual imagery and physical sculpture (see p. 136). The photorealistically rendered image *Forest Devils' Moon Night* (1990) consists of four monumental sculptures – replicas of actual work – exhibited on a strangely textured prairie.

Another form of computer art is the algorithmic painting where original images are converted by software. Once it has undergone the image-processing, the work appears as if painterly techniques had been used, without the artist having intervened at all. The work of Japanese artist Tsuyoshi Yamamoto (above left and right) and of Middlesex Polytechnic student Simon Schofield (left) shows how this technique has been developed.

Sculpture

Because traditional sculpture has always occupied three dimensions, it seems an obvious candidate for development on the computer. However, as with painting, two views seem to be emerging on what computer sculpture should be. On the one hand are those who argue strongly that computing offers an opportunity to dematerialize the object, so that sculpture can be freed from the fetters of gravity and material constraints. The other view is that although the sculptor can benefit from the experimental freedom that is possible thanks to the computer, the end result must still be a physical manifestation of the object, occupying space in the same way as traditional sculpture.

The first form of computer sculpture has the potential to defy certain laws and modify others, using computer graphics techniques to represent surface appearances. Often, techniques similar to those of the engineer are used, and the forms are seen to be evolving; just a snapshot is provided of a particular point on the continuum of a three-dimensional computer modelling system. These sculptures cannot be built in the physical world; they exist only in the abstract world of numbers.

William Latham has begun to deal with some of these issues in his work, but he focuses on explaining his more recent sculpture in terms of biological metaphors. The software contains such functions as 'Mutator', which is used as 'a subjective user interface for the final stage of form design, based on the natural processes of mutation and breeding by marriage, but with the artist-controlled aesthetic selection deciding which forms survive and breed, and which forms die.'[6]

The process of deciding when and in what way the artist should intervene in the making of form is a recurrent theme in computer-generated imaging. In this case, it is quite possible for the computer to decide which forms will live or die, but it would probably make an artistically unacceptable choice. So it is more appropriate for the artist to select, as in the context of traditional sculpture, which forms are suitable as the work emerges. Within the computer, this experience is expressed as menu options, such as 'very good', 'good', 'bad' and 'very bad'. Once a selection has been made, the computer performs the next step in the mutation, based upon the artist's choice, and displays the resulting set of forms.

As with painters, sculptors have divergent views on the computer. Some feel it is useful for generating ideas for sculptural pieces and showing how these might look when installed in specific sites. Others view it as a means to create sculptural form that suspends natural laws and defies gravity, so that the constructions could not 'exist' in any real sense. One proponent of this latter view is the English artist William Latham, who has worked at an IBM Scientific Centre, creating a range of images using specialist solid modelling software. Above: film still showing one of Latham's computer sculptures.

The compression of the whole sculptural process into a set of menu items can be seen as posing a substantial threat to the physical relationship that artists have traditionally had with their materials. It implies a significant reduction in the intimate process of iterative touch and response that has always epitomised
the relationship between sculptor and medium. As in the paint systems, the computer begins to challenge the fundamental assumption that human intervention is required to perform the creative act. The work of Harold Cohen, for example, is exploring the emergence of an autonomous art machine. And if machines can create an artwork by themselves, the question then arises, should there also be machines capable of appreciating art?

The second kind of computer sculpture also makes intellectual demands on the traditional view of what sculpture should be. It uses the computer system to generate ideas and 'place' them in
a specific location. The sculptor can then view the design in its intended location before it is built, and make all the changes necessary to ensure that the design works well on site.

The American sculptor Rob Fisher is one artist who works in this manner. He uses the computer to design very large, intricate installations that are exceptionally complex because of the enormous number of small parts that make up the sculptures.
He says that, in using the computer 'the dialogue that happens between resultant shapes is like a conversation. The intersections produce wonderful second shapes that you can't predict.'[7]

The work of American artist Kenneth Snelson lies somewhere between that of William Latham, whose work is entirely virtual, and that
of Rob Fisher, who uses the computer as a means to design physical sculpture. Snelson is best known for his finely detailed, three-dimensional models generated by computer, which use all the latest rendering techniques. One of his images presents a series of metal poles held in space by taut metal wires, forming a structure of great elegance. It does not just exist on screen; it is also a physical sculpture. However, Snelson's more recent interest in providing a visual mechanism to express complex scientific phenomena, such as the atom, is entirely screen-based. The resulting models resemble medieval war machines rather than descriptions of basic dynamic structures.

Another version of computer sculpture takes a computer model and uses the information to make a physical model of the object, thus providing a three-dimensional hard copy of the screen image, which could be viewed as sculpture. Such works reintroduce some of the physical experience of traditional media, but, as with many other art and design disciplines, computer sculpture suffers from the inability of the machine to deal with 'real-life' experience of real materials. One solution could be the successful development of 'touch and feel' dimensions within the virtual reality field (p. 149).

While these Latham sculptures look as if they are based on some biological image, they are in fact examples of a range of forms that have been adapted by an evolutionary mechanism within the software. Slightly different forms are created by changing some of the variables in the program. It is by tweaking the numbers that Latham produces the final images. Opposite, above left: *Slugan 2*; centre right: *Mutation X*; below left: *Tusk 9*.

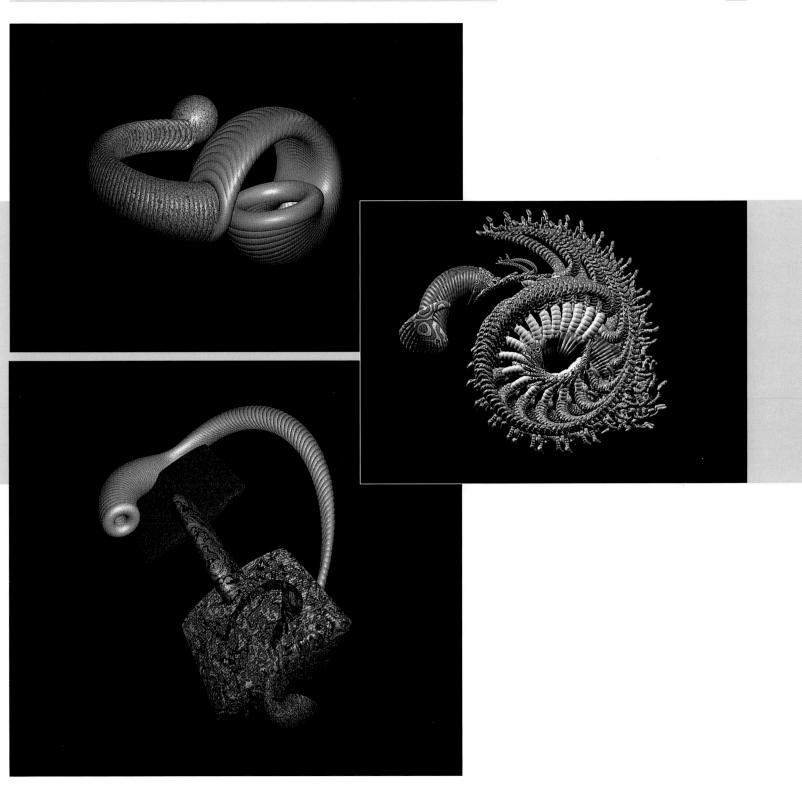

Other artists have used the computer to provide realistic interpretations of sculptural ideas and to place these in a particular context. The three-dimensional modelling system then shows a collection of views, and allows the sculptor to adjust the design until the final form is reached. Rob Fisher, for example, used architectural and scientific visualization software to provide a picture of what his forms would look like when hung in a shopping mall. The sculpture left, *Symphony of the Air*, which is based on flocks of birds, fills the 250 metre-long skylight of the shopping mall with veils of reflection. The computer was able to simulate the views from a variety of locations: from the escalators and elevators, as well as from the main shopping levels.

The strands of all these disciplines are converging, as they increasingly overlap within a digital base. The question therefore arises, is there much point in educating future generations of students as textile designers, graphic designers, architects or industrial designers? Instead of adhering to outmoded nineteenth-century categories, should we not rather be seeking overarching disciplines defined by more general characteristics? The argument is not based on the belief that we need to produce Renaissance men (or women) capable of turning their hands to any aspect of art or design, but purely on a recognition that the convergence of formerly separate disciplines should inform the education and practice of design in creating new and more appropriate structures.

Main picture: screen image of *Fandango*, a computer-assisted environmental sculpture by Rob Fisher. Inset: the real sculpture *in situ*, in Scotsdale, Arizona.

Kenneth Snelson has always been concerned with the visualization of structure. The work shown above is an imagined structure illustrating how atoms stay together. The stones that form the three-dimensional arches are not cemented together, but held in place as in a spherical bridge; the sections are individually pulled towards the centre by spoke-like chains, and their resistance against this compression holds the whole dynamic structure together. Right: atoms at an exhibition of Snelson's work.

4 TRANSFORMING REALITY

The previous chapter described how computing is currently being applied to disciplines as varied as architecture, sculpture and industrial design. Such uses probably represent the major function of computing today within art and design; students and professional designers are intent on using the new technologies to do what they have always done, but with greater efficiency. The problem with this approach is that it does not challenge the envelope that the computer occupies, nor does it necessarily redefine the art or design task that is being undertaken.

Some art and design institutions and some professional design organizations are beginning to discover that a new range of issues emerges when computing is approached as a medium in its own right. This chapter explores what these issues are and how they may begin to change not only how designers do things, but also what they do. The medium of computing throws up the possibility of entirely new disciplines, demonstrating the full potential of the new technologies.

When it is used unconventionally within art and design to explore the limits of what is possible and desirable, the computer provides very fertile ground for the practical and theoretical solutions of the future. The computer as a medium is taking designers into new areas of work that require very different attitudes and skills. To create some pattern, so that they might be better understood, these new areas have been divided into two groups. This division is intended to clarify the contribution they have made to redefining the boundaries of design expertise. However, it could well be that, as the art and design communities begin to interpret and absorb their meaning, elements will cross over from one grouping to another.

The first group of likely new disciplines consists of multimedia, virtual reality, interface or interaction design, and design for visualization. Some designers are already staking a claim for these, as it is likely that they will gradually replace many of today's traditional design disciplines. The second grouping is formed from media that are sufficiently distinct to be considered in their own right. It includes such areas as rapid prototyping, digital publications, shape grammar, genetic algorithms and neural networks. All of these represent particular views of the design future, occupying areas in the overlap between art, design and computing. The way in which they are described in this book therefore provides only a snapshot of their present relationships, which could change dramatically in the future.

THE NEW DESIGN DISCIPLINES

Interaction Design

There are few areas of human activity that have not been affected by the the computer. As its influence spreads, so the relationship between the user and the machine changes, with the user deforming less and the machine more. This evolution is apparent in other technologies, such as the car and the television. The same process of 'humanization' will happen – is happening – to the computer, as it becomes more and more a part of everyday life. The process does not, however, happen automatically. The role of the artist and designer is crucial in seeing that this transition occurs in a way that is not purely technical, but includes aspects of social and cultural behaviour.

Generous financing by many hardware and software suppliers has established research groups to look at different ways in which human/computer interaction can be improved, by making the product easier and more natural to use. Computer developers have largely ignored the need to fit the machine more readily into accepted patterns of human behaviour and link it to the range of tacit knowledge that users have. The artist and designer, however, are well placed to make a significant contribution to this transition from the arcane instrument to the 'human-factored' product. Their inherent visual skills, their ability to synthesize, as opposed to analyse, their understanding of the needs of end-users: these qualities mean that they have a vital role to play in supplementing the efforts of the natural sciences, which have so far failed to provide new and ingenious solutions to the problem of humanizing the technology.

The Graphical User Interface was an early attempt to interact with the computer using techniques other than a keyboard. It enabled the user to navigate through the internal structure of a machine using images and icons, rather than wrestling with complex text- and number-based command line instructions. The original form of the Graphical User Interface, in early Apple Macintosh computers, had other features, such as 'a pointing device – typically a mouse – on-screen menus that appear and disappear on the instruction of the pointer, and windows that graphically display what the computer is doing. In addition, icons were used to represent files, folders and directories, dialogue boxes, buttons, sliders and a host of other functions including a wastebasket.'[1]

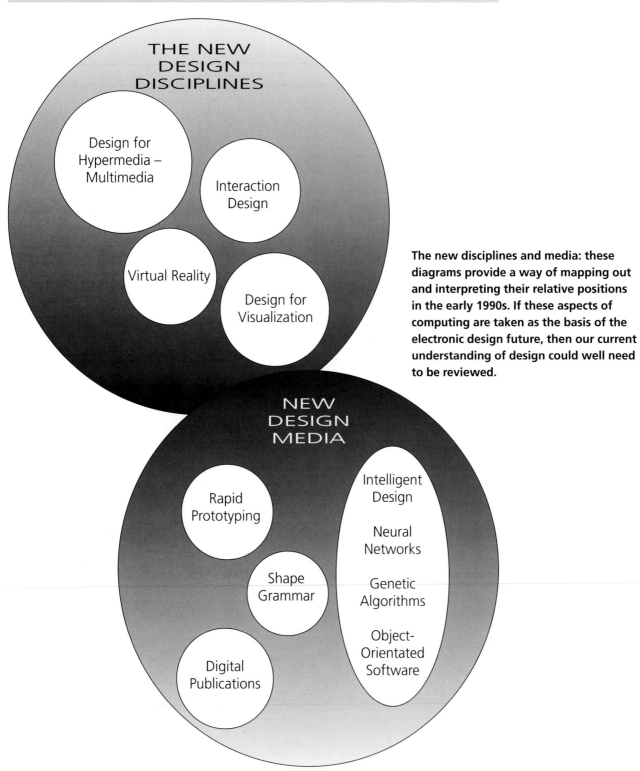

THE NEW
DESIGN
DISCIPLINES

Design for
Hypermedia –
Multimedia

Interaction
Design

Virtual Reality

Design for
Visualization

NEW
DESIGN
MEDIA

Rapid
Prototyping

Intelligent
Design

Neural
Networks

Shape
Grammar

Genetic
Algorithms

Object-
Orientated
Software

Digital
Publications

The new disciplines and media: these diagrams provide a way of mapping out and interpreting their relative positions in the early 1990s. If these aspects of computing are taken as the basis of the electronic design future, then our current understanding of design could well need to be reviewed.

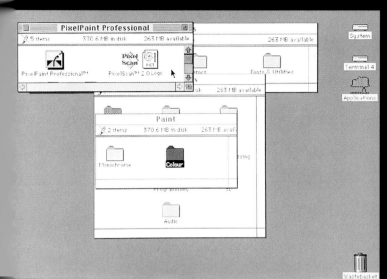

remember very complex codes and to wrestle with long command-line inputs, all the user had to do was to look at the small symbols, or icons, on the screen and select the appropriate one for the task in hand. This system recognized the fact that most people who use computers do not have substantial computing experience. What they do have is many years' direct knowledge of the world around them. The Apple GUI (above and below left) exploits this accumulated experience by making the computer correspond, as nearly as possible, to the everyday world. The whole graphic presentation, which owes a great deal to the early work at Xerox, is aimed at making the computer accessible to the lay person. Because the icons are based on everyday objects, such as folders and dustbins, they are very easy to remember.

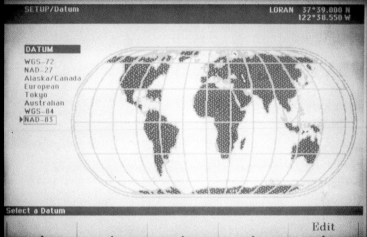

n the early days of computing, before the GUI, the user was required to enter elaborate typed codes and commands to make the computer do something as simple as saving or deleting a file. The method was a direct descendant of the mainframe computer days, when the screen was the exclusive preserve of highly literate computer scientists, and this way of interacting with the computer was perfectly acceptable while only the experts were involved.

In 1981 Xerox developed a new and intuitive method of interaction, called the Star Interface. Instead of having to

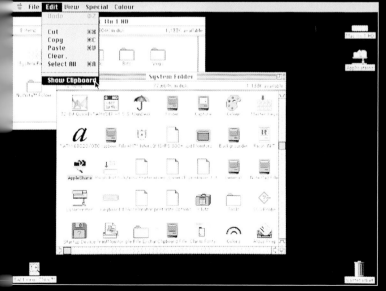

As the GUI was, to an extent, separate from the various applications (wordprocessing, drawing, or three-dimensional modelling) a consistency of use was established. Commands such as 'cut and paste', or the method for selecting a block of text, for example, were the same in many different applications. Several other functions were standard across a range of software, and this consistency gave users sufficient confidence to transfer their skills to other applications. Users familiar with wordprocessing, say, could go on to use a database program and then attempt the construction of a three-dimensional model, because there was a single, straightforward way of doing things that applied to all of the applications. After all, most people do not use computers for the sake of it; they simply want to get a job done. This direct and flexible form of interaction is now firmly established, and today there are many products on the market that use GUIs.

Many versions of the GUI now exist; although they may employ different styles of interaction, they are fundamentally very similar. There are some hybrids, but most consist of 'three major components: a windowing system, an imaging model and an application program interface'.[2]

Since the introduction of the Apple Lisa in 1984, several other GUIs have made an impression on the computer market. Microsoft Windows (below left) has been a major success on the PC, while Hewlett

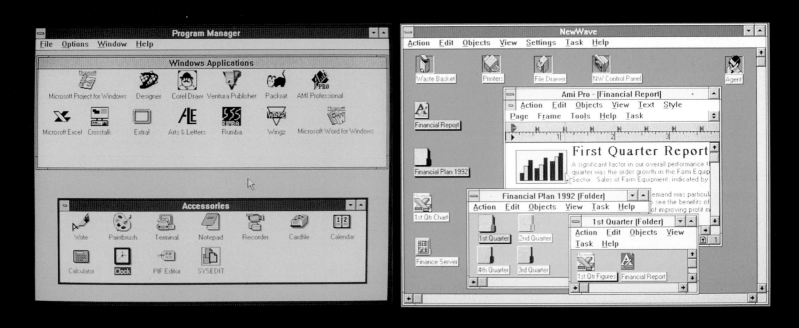

The interface has been described as the place where the user and the computer meet (normally the screen). The less like each other the 'protagonists' are, the more need there is need for an interface to bridge the gap. The traditional interface consisted of hardware and software components, through which the user would communicate with the machine, and the machine communicate with the user. The interface was seen as a physical surface where the interaction took place, as something 'discrete and tangible' that had a physical location. In other words, a physical component was likely to exist. Interaction design, as it is now being defined, no longer sees this as a constraining factor. As computer technology has broadened its domain of use, so the arena of interaction design has expanded. Many disciplines have seen value in contributing to the definition, and designers have also staked a claim for inclusion, since they have the visual skills that are needed.

While the computer was just a tool in the researcher's laboratory, there was no pressure to develop new ways to ease interaction. Scientists knew how to get what they wanted from the machine. However, once the computer had become a ubiquitous tool, with 'ordinary' people using it to perform their work, it was important that the lay person

Packard's New Wave (above right), IBM OS/2's Presentation Manager, Sun's Open Windows (opposite, left), NextStep from Next Computer, and Decwindows from Digital Computers (opposite, right) all seek to establish some form of standard, certainly within their own product line, if not across other computer platforms.

This proliferation of GUIs presents only a limited range of graphical interaction, however. The next-generation development of high-resolution images, input from live video, sound, speech recognition, and other aspects of multi-media, will tend to confuse the issue, unless some form of intelligence – perhaps in the guise of agents – can be included, as part of the move towards more 'natural' computing devices.

should be guided through the minefield of use and functionality, without needing to know about the underlying computational issues.

If products and processes were so clearly designed that users were able to understand intuitively how to use them, then this arena of interaction design would not exist.

Industrial designers have long studied the problem of the human interface with products as part of their general design work, but they have traditionally come up with 'hard' solutions, probably because

However, as everyday objects seem to grow more and more complex, there is an increasing need for designers to take a role in demythologizing the machine. Graphic designers need to apply their traditional skills – combined with an understanding of the new skills and technologies involved – to the representation of information on the computer screen. Skills of layout, the use of colour and type, and the mixing of still and moving images are all necessary to enable the screen to communicate more effectively with the user.

Industrial designers have traditionally dealt with products that require the design of an interface – although it has not been considered in such an explicit manner. When they work on the design of many household products, such as washing machines, microwave ovens and hair dryers, they also have to consider how people use them. But the solutions are largely expressed as hardware. If such issues are not a new problem for the industrial designer, they have traditionally been handled using established design skills, and not addressed as part of a multi-disciplinary team approach.

While these new disciplines do rely on the traditional skills of the designer, these are no longer sufficient in themselves. The problems generated by the microchip require

they have little experience in the area of 'soft' solutions.

In 1988 the Claris Corporation hired the then ID Two design consultancy to work on the interface of the Claris product MacWrite II. Following the successful launch of this product, the Claris Human Interface Group was founded in 1989. Hewlett Packard set up a similar User Interface design group, which provided the Open Software Foundation's Motif interface, HP Vue and then New Wave. Graphic designers now form part of extensive teams involving ergonomicists, psychologists and software writers, all of whom are focused on designing this new area of interaction with the computer.

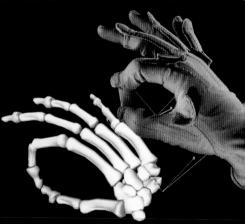

Solutions to the problem of communication between user and computer have not all been software-based. They include a series of gloves, headsets and datasuits that have been designed with the aim of providing more intuitive ways of interacting.

W Industries of the UK have used this new flight-helmet device (above) to provide a virtual reality experience for entertainment, to be used in arcades and leisure centres. These environments can be linked, so that a group of users can explore the VR together. Although these products are being developed within the leisure industries, they could also be used to perform interaction tasks in more day-to-day contexts. Right and opposite, above left: the Cyberglove developed by Virtual Technologies.

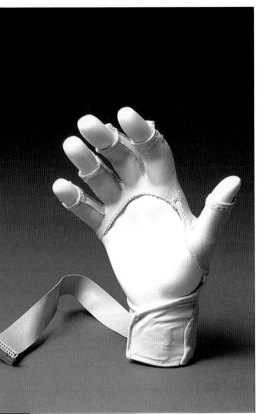

solutions that are far more dense than those used in the past. They raise issues of metaphor, types of representation, cognition, sound, movement, graphics and text – demanding a range of skills that do not normally form part of the design education of graphic and industrial designers. To provide the density of solution that is required, alongside the designer will be the cognitive scientist, the psychologist, the film-maker and the software engineer. Each has a role to play in the design of the interface; each brings particular skills and knowledge to bear on the solution.

Products that encourage new ways of interacting with the computer, such as visors, gloves, headgear and pressure pads, contribute to the potential of this emerging field. Whatever new technological devices are developed, all will require the artist and designer to interpret their use and meaning. Virtual reality, for example, is one area that could soon subsume the currently separate approaches of graphic and industrial design. It requires the interface to become a more comprehensive information environment, in which the 'natural' interface of speech and gesture predominate. By establishing several modes of sensory connection between the machine and the user, this will provide an all-embracing and immersive experience. It could lead to the installation of a ubiquitous computing system at many levels in the everyday world of the user. Allowing the user to call on all those natural means of communication, such as speech, handwriting, expression and gesture, it will, according to journalist Maureen Caudill, 'place the burden of communication squarely on the computer rather than on the human. Instead of the user having to learn the computer's preferred interface, the computer must deal with the user's preferences.'[3]

Virtual Reality

As with many of the new disciplines within which design has a role to play, there is no substantive or agreed definition that can describe virtual reality in neat and comprehensible terms. 'Virtual reality refers to the ability to computer-generate realistic three-dimensional worlds that the operator can explore and interact with through natural interfaces such as the glove and helmet': such working definitions describe the components, but not the experience. If we aim at a consensus view, then the definition

The idea of using a computer to simulate an environment, object or process in order to gain greater insight into it has been developing for some time in a range of disciplines. The computer simulation of architecture, for example, has become an established tool, with ever-increasing realism being achieved. Views from Nashville, a computer perspective of San Francisco produced to commemorate the opening of new offices in the Bay area, illustrates this trend.

becomes so general as to include any medium that simulates a real or imaginary world by electronic means and allows the viewer to participate in it.

This lack of an adequate definition derives from the fact that virtual reality has moved from the pages of science fiction to the laboratory, and then to the market at such a pace that the product was in existence before there had been time to absorb it into the culture. Many designers do not understand what virtual reality is or what it can do. This confusion is intensified because many of the products that have been demonstrated, although still in the prototype stage, show, very forcibly, what the convergence of traditional forms of computing could begin to provide for the user. Three-dimensional graphics, animation, interface design, parallel processing, sound and tactile feedback all exist as separate areas of development; their linking has enabled virtual reality to develop very quickly, firing the imagination of the scientific and artistic community, as well as exciting much media attention.

The idea of using, first, mechanical methods and then computers to simulate events or locations is not new. It received considerable backing from the military, who saw that such techniques could provide ideal training for tactical battle situations, without using expensive military hardware or endangering life. In the commercial field, simulation has been employed by a variety of professionals, including architects, engineers and planners, and within the civil aircraft industry. Most of these simulations have concentrated on the visual component, allowing limited interaction along a linear path.

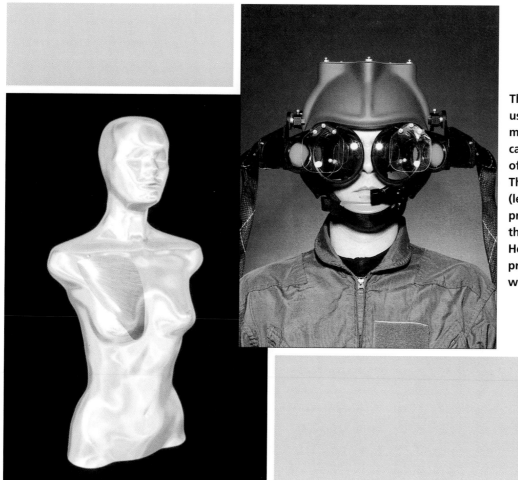

The image of a woman's torso (far left) is used in an educational video describing methods for detecting and treating breast cancer. It illustrates just one potential use of simulation for the medical profession. The fibre-optic helmet-mounted display (left), developed by CAE Electronics, projects computerized information on to the windows in front of the user's eyes. Head- and eye-tracing techniques enable presentation of very detailed scenes in whichever direction the user looks.

To make the simulated experience as 'real' as possible, much effort has been expended in creating, through computer graphics, a visually realistic representation, to the exclusion of most other human senses. Initial work on virtual reality began to correct this imbalance by creating a synthetic computer environment that, while remaining predominately visual, demonstrated how sound and touch could also be incorporated. The main difference between a computer simulation and a virtual reality experience is that VR makes an ambitious attempt to map many more of the human senses on to the machine, creating a more convincing representation of real-life experience.

The fundamental contribution of VR is that it allows users to feel they are within the system, rather than outside it, as in the case of a traditional computer system – a concept that has been described by science-fiction writers for many decades. Users find themselves among the images, moving things around, experiencing an immersive, all-round involvement; they are placed at the very centre of things.

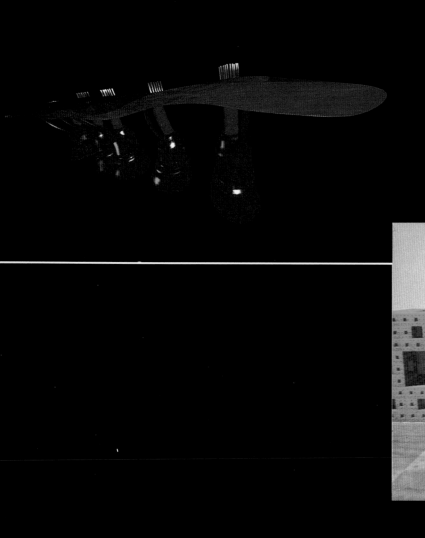

Scientific experiments and simulations provide visually complex images that have considerable aesthetic appeal. This form of scientific visualization can be seen as a direct development of early experiments with the computer and pen plotter. Now the images produced by scientists are in full colour and take advantage of the latest rendering and animation techniques.

To remove some of the awkwardness of suiting and de-suiting associated with head-mounted viewers, Fake Space Laboratories of California developed the BOOM (Binocular Omni-Orientated Monitor), a counterbalanced, CRT-based stereoscopic viewer (right). This enables users to enter and exit from the virtual world quickly, and so makes real-world tasks easy to integrate with virtual tasks. The use of the BOOM viewer to examine a numerical aerodynamic simulation of dynamic data in a virtual wind tunnel demonstrates that such devices are ideally suited to practical tasks, such as scientific visualization.

The entertainment industries have used early virtual reality techniques to create immersive computer games. These two examples are typical of VR leisure centres in both Europe and the USA.

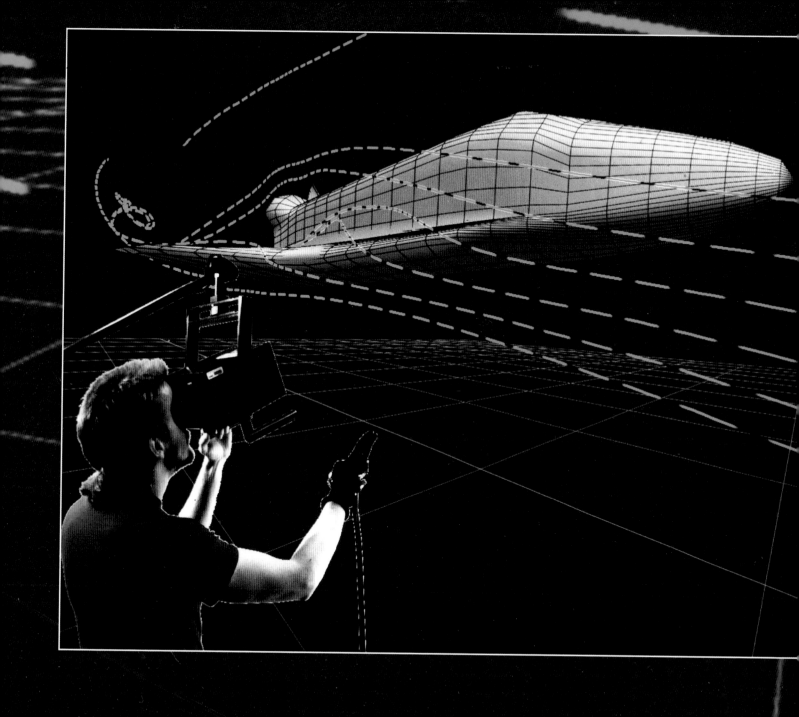

Below: BOOM viewer in use at the Fake Space Labs. Right and bottom: Jeffrey Shaw's interactive display *Legible City* simulates the experience of cycling through a city constructed of letters, words and sentences. The cyclist can move through the city at will, turning left or right, and controlling the speed by pedalling faster or slower. The streets are constructed as three-dimensional letters, which become words and sentences as the cyclist moves along between them. They conform to the actual street plans of New York or Amsterdam, following well-known thoroughfares, crossing bridges and forming intersections.

The most dramatic techniques of VR are the headsets, datagloves and datasuits, which allow the user to cut off from the everyday world and enter the virtual world. The use of articles of clothing, such as masks, gloves and suits, as a means of connection to the computer system, demonstrates that the 'natural interface' is beginning to appear as a working prototype. It is natural in the sense that gloves and headsets are familiar objects linked to everyday experience, so the user has some idea of how to use them. These traditional objects have been given a new meaning within VR. They have become not only the means of interacting with the machine, by using many aspects of the human sensory system, but also immediately understandable icons of interaction.

The other development that virtual reality has provided is an electronic environment that will allow participation by a number of users simultaneously. Provided that all the players don the headsets and datagloves, they can be represented – and not only as themselves, but as anything they wish – in this 'Alice in Wonderland' world.

How will virtual reality be used? What are the skills needed to use it, and to what extent are these transferable to the 'real' world? Such questions are bound to arise when technology can simulate almost anything the designer wishes. Entertainment seems one early use. Arcade game and theme park promoters see in virtual reality an ideal tool for providing ever more intense experiences, while avoiding the space problem of traditional theme park rides. The self-contained VR game can provide a virtual ride on any subject within the small space occupied by the computer.

Many scientific projects have taken advantage of virtual reality to interact with information in new ways. In the virtual world, three-dimensional steady state flows can be explored from the inside, and three-dimensional molecules can be combined manually. Clinical diagnostics is another area in which VR has significant implications for the future. Computer graphics can provide models of an individual's anatomy, which can then be scaled and positioned to provide the most appropriate view. One major near-term goal is telecollaboration. Japanese electronics companies have already developed a VR network that enables designers to work together while they are in physically different locations, simultaneously handling three-dimensional solids for the design of a car body. In the visual arts, too, virtual reality can demonstrate interactive environments which are beginning to redefine what computer art could include.

Design for Process Data Visualization

All computer graphics can be seen at one level as the visualization of data. A computer painting, a piece of animation, a three-dimensional model and a computer wireframe drawing are all based on a series of numerical values. They are images of what data looks like, and the data is specifically generated to make the image.

The difference in process data visualization is that either the data already exists, or the researcher needs to interact with it to see what happens when certain variables are changed. In both cases the skill lies in making the data into some meaningful visual form by making the process that generated the data visible. Data can only be turned into useful information if some intelligence is applied to it, so that the outcome becomes meaningful. The purpose of computing, as computer scientist Richard Hamming observed, is insight, not numbers.

This new technique stems from the increasing use of various kinds of sensors, satellites, video cameras and data-loggers, all of which can capture information, often indiscriminately, at a rapid rate and over a prolonged period. The problem is that the capture of that information far outstrips its assimilation by the scientific community. The now famous 1987 report by the US National Science Foundation describes the problem in graphic detail: 'Today's data sources are such firehoses of information that all we can do is gather and warehouse the numbers they generate.'

The problem is further exacerbated by the computer's rapid development, which through continual technological innovation allows analysis of ever finer problems, thereby adding more and more data. Weather prediction is one example of this explosion of data: 'until this past generation of supercomputers, computational scientists could not solve three-dimensional models; they could only solve two-dimensional slice models. Therefore, even generating simple models, such as the weather above the North American continent, people twenty-five years ago would compute three layers of weather, then five layers, then seven layers. But now, we begin to deal with many layers. Instead of just visualizing it as three sheets, one has to visualize it as a volume of results that the computational model has produced.'[4]

In many areas of the computational sciences – medicine, astrology, molecular biology – there are two types of bottleneck in dealing with information. The first is to some extent solvable, where researchers need to analyse existing data that has been building up over a period of time, in order to decide on further courses of action. The second requires a more dynamic approach, as scientists need to conduct their experiments in a way they have not been able to do so far, because the technology has not been sufficiently sophisticated. The researchers need to interpret the data and modify the experiment *during* the calculation through some form of iterative and interactive visual computing. They wish to be able to 'steer' an experiment while it is being performed in order to direct the work towards new objectives. The only clear solution, in something like 'real time', is to provide a visualization of the particular experiment in such a way that the principal notions are clearly monitored and unambiguously displayed at regular intervals. To some extent, this puts the scientist in the computing loop. The user is placed at the centre of the information, rather than acting as some distant observer.

The 'information-without-interpretation' dilemma is not confined to the scientific community. Such issues also arise in the business community, where it is estimated that current computer and organizational systems can handle only about 20 per cent of the data that is being produced. This is not a static situation, as the raw data is continuously

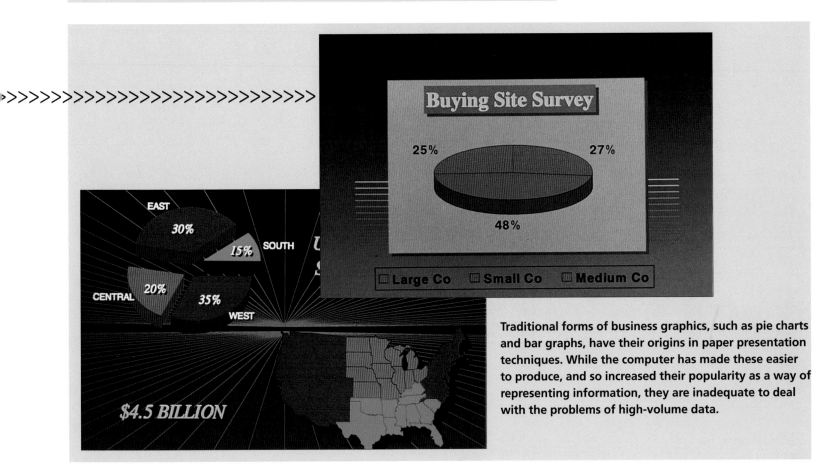

Traditional forms of business graphics, such as pie charts and bar graphs, have their origins in paper presentation techniques. While the computer has made these easier to produce, and so increased their popularity as a way of representing information, they are inadequate to deal with the problems of high-volume data.

being churned out by computers that are growing larger and faster, and which have the potential to generate even more data.

Business visualization is closely related to scientific visualization, and uses similar tools for a similar purpose – to extract some potentially significant trend or development from reams of data. The sheer amount of information to be processed in actuarial tables and demographic statistics, for example, militates against its elucidation. Trends cannot easily be spotted until there is a visual equivalent that can interpret the data and communicate hidden developments to the user. Currency and securities traders also wish to interact in real time with real, if not live, data within the market, so that they can see the results of different interventions, and decide on appropriate action.

Data-overload is not a new problem, but it is one to which designers are beginning to turn their attention – particularly designers who have a background in computing and skills in graphic information design, as well as animation. Traditional computer tools for looking at data are unable to cope with the quantities with which they now have to deal, so it is necessary to move into a new arena, where human perceptual skills are linked to computational processes. Multimedia and virtual reality probably have an increasing role

to play in this context, and the new design skills can also be applied to the problem, as they represent a unique combination of traditional skills and recent perceptions. The design solution will probably not resemble conventional bar charts, pie charts or line graphs – the visual techniques that have been promoted in much business graphics software. Animation techniques are just some of the design skills that could be used to clarify rapidly changing relationships, and to represent the complexity of information that alters almost instantaneously.

Another development that could be driven by the visual designers is the use of sound to accompany and clarify the expression of complex sets of data. Often, background music is attached to visualizations, but how much more productive could be sound that is generated directly by the information itself. Scientific and business visualization has begun to move into mainstream computer graphics with the aim of displaying the unseen, of being able to show the user what lies hidden in multivariate data. It is not inconceivable that as well as 'seeing' data, it would be possible to hear it, and perhaps also to apply other senses to help clarify an interpretation. It would be interesting to hear what a spreadsheet sounds like. The use of an additional channel of interpretation to

New interactive methods for displaying data are being developed that provide users with many ways of interacting with the information, allowing them to choose what kind of information they wish to see. This design represents London Stock Exchange data, which can be viewed over time, so that trends can be determined and integrated with various other items of financial news and information. It is designed as a virtual world, and the user is intended to be able to view the data from 'inside'.

enhance the visual dimension would perhaps offer the user a greater understanding of both the form of analysis and the content of the data.

A new group of users will eventually benefit from these data-analysing techniques, including economists, academics, managers and business people, as well as the scientific community. Ultimately, anyone using data could gain from the benefits of visualization.

Interactive Multimedia

As we have already seen, the development of the computer is potentially as important as the invention of printing, and until now, it is the book that has largely determined how information has been structured. Books are convenient, relatively inexpensive, and can be printed in their thousands. They are so well integrated into our culture that many collect them. Because the book holds this dominant position, it has been able to impose a particular method on the delivery of ideas, facilitating the acceptance of its linear tradition by a complete culture. Film, radio and then television all inherited this linear approach to information, and continued to assume that authorship automatically conveyed the right to control the means of transmission. That is to say, the reader had little control over the content of a book, or the viewer over the content, length or timing of a film. This limitation has been accepted as part of our culture, as something to do with the very nature of film, books, plays and television.

Although each of the traditional media building blocks (books, television etc.) had a rich texture, it was understood that they could only be delivered in isolation. This fragmentation is very unlike our experience of everyday life, which provides a seamless context for their delivery, in that the reader or viewer acts as a link between the disparate blocks of information. However, there seemed to be no other way of combining the information contained in a novel with that of a television series, or images from a slide set with a film – or, indeed, all four. Their very diversity and separate means of delivery kept them apart. All this seemed quite natural until new technology was able to demonstrate that this structure could be overturned.

Apart from the computer, the major item of popular hardware that destroyed the tyranny of the broadcaster was the video cassette recorder. This allowed individual recording of television programmes and broke the broadcasters' control over scheduling, by allowing users to watch programmes whenever they wished, to stop them and replay them on demand. Choosing which piece to skip by fast-forwarding, which section to see again by using the replay function, users can now be more selective about what they watch and when they watch it. More control is placed in the hands of the receiver of information, and less in the hands of the deliverer.

This represents a significant shift in the control of information, as it places less focus on how information is sent, and much more on how it is sought. People are thus put back in the driving seat of technology. The importance of interaction is underlined, removing

Thatcher's cylindrical slide rule, patented in 1881, has over 33,000 divisions printed on its surface. To match this accuracy a 20-metre conventional slide rule would have to be used.

This computer, known as the Whirlwind II, was developed at MIT in the late 1950s. It was used by the military to create a Semi-Automatic Ground Environment (SAGE), which formed part of the US air defence system.

much of the passivity associated with conventional television, for example. The idea that the user could structure and then restructure visual information was a conceptual breakthrough. It broadened the traditional view of the media and raised the question of how much more information was editable within the computer.

The modern computer was essentially developed according to the nineteenth-century notion that it should be able to process large volumes of data and perform accurate and reliable calculations at high speed. Military use of the early vacuum tube computers accelerated their development, and provided a conceptual framework that was extended to other forms of information storage and retrieval.

One such idea was developed during the 1940s, in the USA, by the now famous Vannevar Bush, who constructed an imaginative system called 'Memex'. In his 1945 article[5] he outlined a procedure for organizing and accessing the increasing amount of research data that was accumulating. The major new concept that he proposed – together with that of information storage and retrieval – was 'associative indexing'.

This demonstrated how two or more pieces of information could be tied together, or 'tagged'. The user could then make a path through the other data establishing further associations, so adding to the original information as required.

It was to be some time before such a system existed, but the idea was developed by Ted Nelson for his project 'Xanadu', and has achieved a software implementation with the now popular 'Hypertext' systems (p. 52). The idea behind Hypertext is that the content of many documents can be linked as the user jumps between them, taking relevant elements from each as the search continues. This non-sequential approach, although attempted in the context of traditional media, was never a real possibility before the computer. When applied to images, graphics, video and sound it produces a new interrelationship that has been termed 'multimedia'.

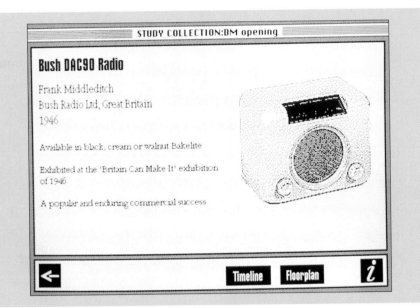

STUDY COLLECTION:DM opening

Bush DAC90 Radio

Frank Middleditch
Bush Radio Ltd, Great Britain
1946

Available in black, cream or walnut Bakelite

Exhibited at the 'Britain Can Make It' exhibition of 1946

A popular and enduring commercial success

Timeline Floorplan *i*

In Bill Atkinson's Hypercard (left) the associative links transport users around the information network, enabling them to connect with a range of media.

Right: Apple's Renaissance project developed the educational potential of multimedia with its presentation of Shakespeare's *Twelfth Night* (1990). A Thames Television tape of the play was used as the basis for live video, and the entire text of the play was transferred to the computer. In addition, the sound track of the play was recorded separately, as were details concerning the Globe Theatre, and contemporary commentaries on the theatre and the historical background to the play. A standard television performance of *Twelfth Night* would be experienced as a linear narrative. Interaction would only be possible if the performance were recorded, so that sections could be replayed when the meaning was unclear, or when the viewer wanted to hear them repeated.

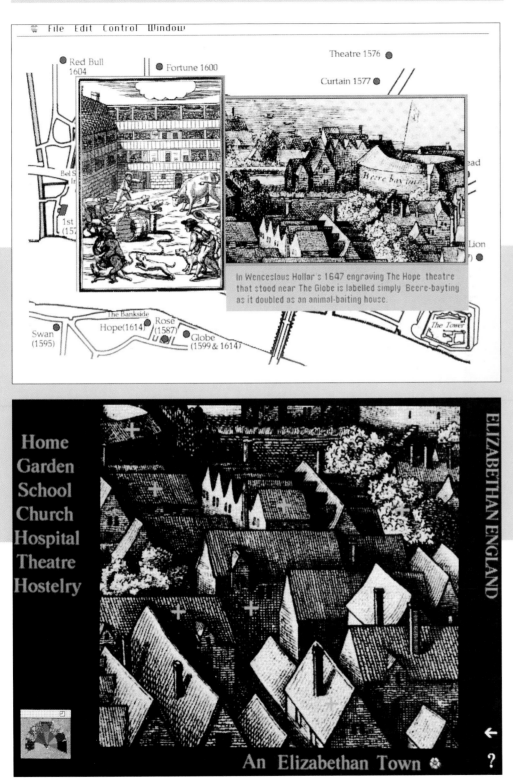

Within the Renaissance multimedia project it is possible to have one computer window (an area of the screen) showing the video performance, while another scrolls the text of the play. When an unfamiliar word occurs, it is possible to stop the play by highlighting the word, and in another window an explanation will appear with annotated references. The context of the play can be explored via a window that displays commentaries on the play and details of relevant contemporary events.

Thus, previous aspects of computing have resurfaced to create the conceptual framework of multimedia. According to Max Whitby, director of the Multimedia Corporation in London, 'A defining characteristic of interactive multimedia is that it allows the consumer to intervene in the presentation of information and to divert the flow or adjust the level of detail according to his or her interest and experience. This very process of intervention seems inevitably to break the spell of engagement with linear media.'[6]

The ability to interconnect traditional, media-rich materials is of potential value to many areas, including education, training, business and entertainment. As the range of existing material that can be incorporated is extensive, multimedia can be seen as a form of hybrid, combining the advantages of existing media with the new potential of the computer.

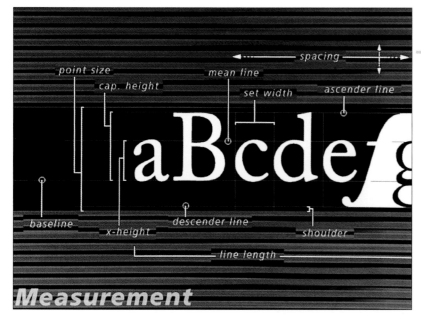

This program for teaching the basic principles of typography uses similar techniques, allowing non-designers to experiment with those aspects of the tutorial that suit their needs and abilities.

However, this raises a whole set of issues for the conventional publishing business. Kristina Hooper Woolsey, director of Apple computers' Multimedia Laboratory in San Francisco, explains: 'We know how the book trade works. Acquisition editors go out, find the content people, and fold them into a time-tested and well-worn publishing system.... Multimedia, by contrast, is currently far-flung and chaotic ... as publishers have to worry not only about production/manufacturing, but also about the hardware that serves their products.... How will multimedia publishers sell their products in the future?'[7]

Although interactive multimedia seems an ideal use for the electronic computer, it does raise certain problems. One of these involves the difficulty of navigating around such a non-traditional space. The non-linear approach means that users must be able to find where they are in the new electronic space, so the notion of electronic guides, or agents,

These two examples show different uses of multimedia, the first intended for production as a CD-I, and the second as a television programme. The dance tutorial, called 'Ceroc', allows viewers to practise a French rock-and-roll dance. The various moves can be examined and replayed, and then copied, so that the basic dance is learned interactively. The interface is modelled on a 1950s jukebox. The second project, *Architecture as Navigation,* uses the metaphors of a Boullée lighthouse and a horse for navigating around a gallery of computer luminaries.

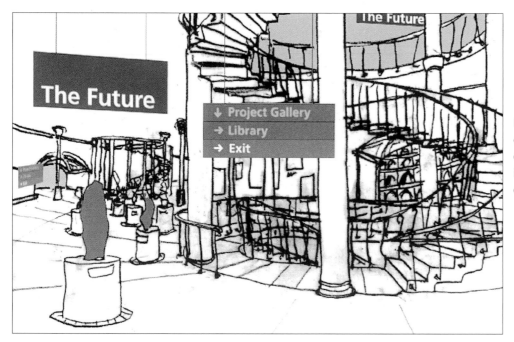

The Future

↓ Project Gallery
→ Library
→ Exit

In the case of the architectural metaphor employed in *Architecture as Navigation* doors and windows function just as they do in real buildings, allowing access to differing kinds of information.

could well prove vital. As the potential for multimedia develops, the scale of the information environment to which the user can gain access is going to increase to the scale envisaged in 'Xanadu'. Users will simply become lost and frustrated if they do not feel confident in browsing, or, alternatively, in being able to navigate purposefully towards their objective.

As a result of such activities, there could come into play another factor that is essentially founded in the electronic environment: the user as composer. In the same way that in Hypertext, words, sentences or whole paragraphs can be labelled as 'hot', indicating that they are associated with further items of information, different media – television, video or film – could be linked together to provide additional material or a more detailed explanation. This would allow for interactive media to be 'composed' into a form that has meaning and value for the user. By constructing their own programs, users will be involved in the process of creation, as well as in that of consumption.

Developments that may follow from the emergence of the interactive multimedia discipline include 'Hypervideo' systems based on the Hypertext idea, but using video sequences rather than words. Another possibility is the linking of multimedia databases to spreadsheets, termed 'Hypercalc'; this uses numbers more interactively, by establishing the rules that link conditions to actions.

Interactive multimedia requires a rather different combination of skills from that provided by traditional design education. It requires the composition of a very complex task, using video or film sequences, still images, text, graphics and animation, all of which are computer-controlled. The nearest skills are those of the film-maker or television producer, although the limitations of linear narrative are often built into their vision of the world, and they often lack computational skills.

Nevertheless, the art and design disciplines are the nearest in spirit to the needs of interactive multimedia. If designers are to adopt this discipline as their own, a fusion of old and new skills must take place. The new skills that will have to be developed are those that deal with what has been termed 'repurposing'[8] – using material originally created for an entirely different purpose in a way that solves the current problem. Much information used in the creation of interactive multimedia products tends to have been made initially for other reasons. The potential recycling of information therefore becomes an important aspect.

As with many other emerging electronic disciplines, such as virtual reality, there is a problem in defining what precisely interactive multimedia is, or even if it exists at all. Whatever view is taken depends on the observer.

For practical purposes, multimedia can be defined as the combining of graphics, sound, scanned images, text and video in an interactive way, enabling the user to extract meaning for a particular need in a non-linear fashion. But beyond listing the components in this way, any definition is still very problematical. One reason is that multimedia software and hardware products have already been in the marketplace for some time. As is typically the case with many of the new technologies, products are designed, prototyped and distributed before there has been time to understand them fully or to provide them with agreed meanings. As John Sculley, chief executive officer of Apple computers, puts it, 'The problem with the term Multimedia is that it's too high a level of abstraction. I don't know what it means. Is it a market? Is it a technology? Television, which connotes vision and communications at a distance, is more descriptive than multimedia. Maybe we don't have to change the name. Maybe it's just a question of learning what multimedia is as we start to experience it?'[9]

THE NEW DESIGN MEDIA

Of the new design media that have been selected for discussion here, it is interesting to note that all involve some level of 'understanding', on the part of the computer, of what it is processing. While wishing to make no special claims for this emphasis, it is clear that the new design media are drawing on aspects of artificial intelligence to find ways in which the computer might aid the designer. There is little doubt that this perspective will yield very useful new computational tools. However, the intention here is simply to sketch their outline and, where possible, to illustrate the visual results that some have already achieved.

Most computer-aided design systems have elaborate modelling and drawing facilities, rapid rendering capacity, and are very fast calculators. But they are, for the most part, unintelligent. The computer is not only blind and deaf, but is also unaware of what it is doing, as it slavishly obeys the instructions of the user to produce a photorealistic rendering of a design object.

Work has been carried out to try to change the situation, by providing the computer with information that it can interpret in a way that allows it to act autonomously, or 'intelligently'. In knowledge-based engineering, for example, this would mean providing rules that captured the geometric description of a class of objects. The particular parameters of a specific design would be entered, and the computer would consult the rules and design the object according to the programmed parameters.

Another area of application is computer-aided drafting and design. Here, there is an increasing need for the system to understand what it is doing, so that it can, in a marketing sense, be distinguished from a simple electronic drawing board. This form of intelligence, rather than seeking merely to automate the design process, enhances the designer's role by advising on what options are available, so that the user can decide on what action to take. Examples that couple knowledge with geometry are beginning to appear in the software products of major vendors. These work by guiding the designer through drafting and dimensioning, and then 'learning' from his or her actions, so that the next session of work can be geared specifically to the user's abilities or needs. The software is designed to pick up how a person works, to note the kind of mistakes that are made consistently, the speed at which they draw, and so on. At the next session the computer will spend time explaining the mistakes that it has identified, pacing its explanation to the speed at which the computer feels the designer is best able to learn. The computer therefore guides the user, establishing a particular speed and level for each individual. This is often helpful, for example, in computer-assisted language learning. Systems such as these are migrating to the personal computer as the software becomes more efficient, and they will without doubt soon be found in most of the software drawing, drafting and modelling packages used by designers.

In addition, examples of this kind of intelligent system are appearing in process planning and estimation software. A particular class of parts is analysed detail by detail, and the software is then able to determine what tools and processes are necessary for their manufacture, and generate a cost estimate.

The problem with such an approach is that it is necessary to understand, in a very detailed way, what each step in the design process looks like, by breaking down the activity into discrete and sequential units. Most commercial organizations are unable to do this, as their design processes have grown up over many years of successful working, and are so complex as to defy this form of reduction. Neither do they have the necessary in-house computational skills. The market for an 'intelligent' approach to software will therefore remain limited, until there are more efficient ways of understanding how organizations design, and how they can take advantage of added value. Nevertheless, this time will come.

The work of R.A. and J.L. Kirsch is an important contribution to the computer understanding of shape. They succeeded in getting the computer to produce an image without putting a specific one in. Their intention was to demonstrate how the storage capacity of a computer could be used in a more intelligent way if the 'rules' that created a class of images could be stored, rather than the images themselves. In order to do this, they had to break down the original image into a series of rules, which when applied by the computer could construct a number of designs with the look and feel of the original. This technique, called shape grammar, produces a schematic representation that can be understood by both people and machines. Artists like Joan Miró, to whom shape was essential, are ideal candidates for this exercise. The artificial Miró (right) has many of the visual characteristics of the originals.

Shape Grammar

In many design disciplines – but most frequently in architecture – there has been a desire to understand what constitutes a form: what are the component parts? How do they fit together, and what are the other possible relationships?

A computer technique drawn from computational linguistics was applied to the understanding and development of visual form. It is termed 'shape grammar' – a name that represents its roots in both images and language. Our everyday language can be broken down into various rules that underlie and organize its use. Computer systems are also based on rules, and complex problems can be handled when a series of rules is used, as is evident from recent work in artificial intelligence. Of particular interest to designers are *shape rules*. A collection of related shape rules forms a *shape grammar*, and, as a natural extension of this idea, any designs that are the result of applying both shape rules and shape grammar constitute a *shape language*.

Shape rules are simple and define basic transformations, but the range and number of rules employed to create a complex design may be very large. Although pre-computer attempts were made to implement such rules manually, it was not until the advent of the computer that the full potential of this new medium began to be appreciated. The idea of an underlying 'language' structure has been used as a metaphor for the visual arts, and has resulted in a series of studies of particular paintings, buildings and furniture designs. The computer software was able to describe accurately large classes of objects using a linear, visual vocabulary. It not only reconstructed these objects or paintings, but produced a range of alternative objects with a strong family resemblance. Sometimes these were indistinguishable from the originals, because the rules of the grammar mean that there is the potential for most objects to be recreated, theoretically in the style of the original.

Shape grammar does not simply contribute a conceptual device for the analysis and synthesis of objects, paintings and buildings. It could also be used in an innovative way, to teach the history of art, architecture and artefacts, for example; objects could be disassembled in order to understand the rules that underlie them, and then alternatives could be created by putting the same rules into operation.

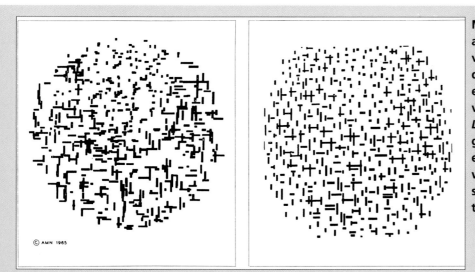

Many researchers have been concerned with the attempt to represent original works of art using various computational techniques, without actually drawing or painting the image. Michael Noll experimented with a semi-random technique on variations of Piet Mondrian's *Composition with Lines* of 1917. Several alternative compositions were generated in the style of Mondrian (left) and then exhibited. Viewers were asked to identify which was the original. Only 28 per cent were able to select the original work, while 59 per cent preferred the computer-generated drawing.

Similar techniques have been used in architecture to create a series of plans from a simple formula. This range of plan forms was constructed at Hong Kong Polytechnic with direction from William Fawcett. They are made up of individual components that are combined in varying configurations. The process is rather like selecting items from a catalogue of parts. The major difference is that in the shape grammar, the rules for selection have to be explicitly stated, whereas an architect could make a visual selection of components from a catalogue – windows, doors etc. – using implicit criteria that would never need to be formally stated.

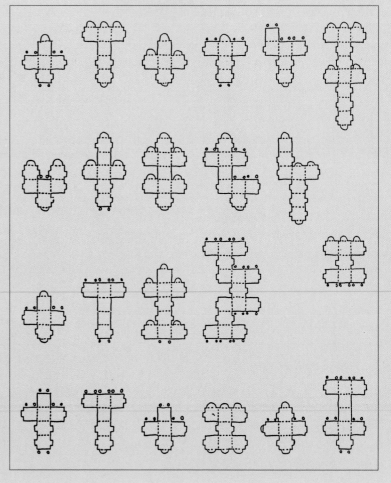

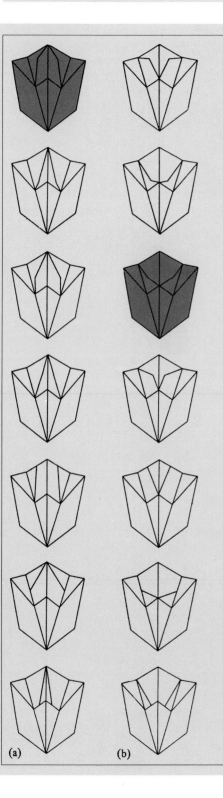

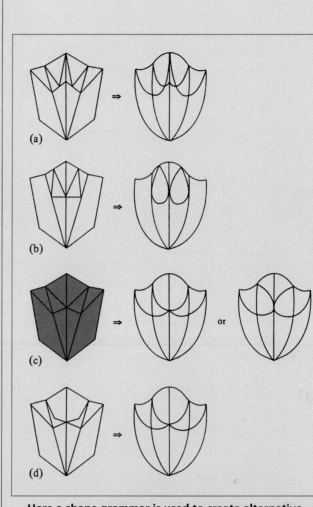

Here a shape grammar is used to create alternative shapes for Hepplewhite-style chairbacks. This kind of form-generation technique is best used when design is considered as a refinement, requiring an alternative set of solutions to be developed from an accepted model.

Object-orientated Programming

Object-orientated programming is named after the way in which the software attempts to represent objects as they appear and behave in the real world. This approach differs from the traditional way in which software has been written – for the efficiency of the computer processor. Being process-orientated, it has tended to be more suited to the machine than to the end-users. In addition, software was developed as a craft-based activity, with a unique individual problem being solved each time. As a result, software may often be written over and over again to solve very similar problems, with no attempt to reuse code from previous applications. The way in which the software is written also makes only a passing acknowledgment to the task that is to be solved in the real world.

Object-orientated programming turns this approach on its head. It starts with an understanding of a real-world problem, and then translates it into appropriate code. The traditional approach is dominated by the language of the machine; with the new development in programming, the process starts at the user's end. Computer journalist John Samson pinpoints the change that has occurred: 'It [object orientation] approaches the design of an application in a way that is diametrically opposite to conventional third-generation programming. The way most of us learned and still practise programming is to think of the processor as an active agent that, according to a prerecorded list of instructions, pulls values out of named pigeonholes, manipulates them in some way and puts them back in the pigeonholes. This mental image has one major advantage. It corresponds well with the way processors actually work. But it has one huge disadvantage too; namely, it is not how human beings normally approach a problem.'[10]

From this change of attitude have followed other ideas that seem to give support to the new approach. Programmers do not want to have to write code each time there is a particular problem to solve, as the economics of the current situation militates against this. So object-orientated programming has introduced the idea of reusable code designed as modules. No designer would consider that with each new problem it is necessary to start at the beginning and reinvent the wheel. In architecture and many other areas of design solutions can frequently be constructed from various standard components – an approach that provides both design flexibility and huge cost savings. Until recently, the position in programming strongly resembled that in design before the Industrial Revolution, when each solution had to be crafted as an individual item. This approach became untenable in an increasingly competitive environment, and it was not a healthy position for a supposedly maturing activity. New developments have shown that software writing is by no means an arcane activity immune to market forces.

The process of design can be seen as a series of ever-decreasing loops, in which each solution put forward is tested against a set of criteria, then revised and tested again until the designer is satisfied with the result. Another advantage of object-orientated programming is that it uses a method of iteration that is very similar to this.

Programming has always been an issue of dispute amongst those designers and artists who consider that the learning of programming languages is unnecessary, as there are already sufficient applications to cover most needs. The opposite camp consists of those who believe that the creative act begins at the software level, and that the artist, in particular, must be able to handle the tools of the trade so as to be able to leave an individual mark. The technique of iteration in object-orientated programming, introduced at differing stages of the design software, represents real-world activities that can be understood at a conceptual level. If artists and designers need to program, then they may be happier working with software that to some extent represents their own working methods.

Genetic Algorithms

Another area of software development that holds potential for art and design is the computer algorithm based on an evolutionary process – or genetic algorithms, as they are now called. This approach was developed in the 1970s, when the workings of biological evolution were used as a model for software design. Such software solves quite simple biological problems by emulating evolutionary processes, so that the solutions become increasingly apposite, the longer the software is allowed to run. It goes through many 'generations', each time providing an answer that is an improvement on the previous solution. In the biological world the improvement factor is judged by the environment in a simple Darwinian sense; but in the software, an additional 'sieve' is used to judge the increased applicability of the solution against a real-world problem, to check that it is a better 'fit' than the previous answer.

The aim of the algorithm is to produce a 'better' solution each time, and in this sense it mimics the biological process very closely. It is very useful for looking at problems that are far too complex to be handled in any other way. In the field of biochemistry, for example, the 'Meta Dendral' software was used to generate new rules for analysing molecules. Another example is given by Suran Goonatilake: 'The artificial intelligence group of the Lockheed Aeronautical Systems group had used genetic algorithms in the parametric design of aircraft. The task involves finding compatible configurations of wing sizes, fuselages, tail lengths and engines for a given class of aircraft. It is an extremely difficult problem, where as many as thirty parameters may be under consideration.'[11]

When dealing with a design problem like this, design engineers would normally reduce the number of variables to a more manageable level. They would, in other words, take a two-dimensional slice of a problem that could in fact occupy a thirty-dimensional space. Genetic algorithms enable solutions to be evolved that are not so simplistic as to be useless, or so complex as to be impractical. The method by which they evaluate solutions is of major interest, as this often takes up the most of the processing time, which can now be very extensive, running into several days of processing.

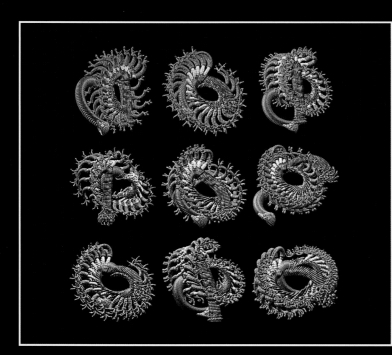

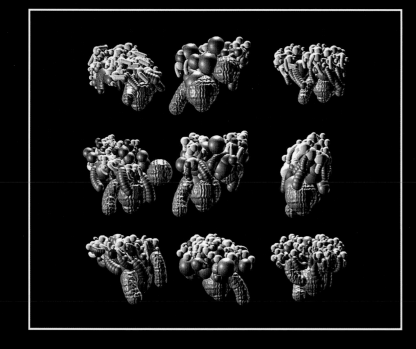

The Mutator software provides a series of nine images that resemble each other, from which the user selects the most artistically pleasing. This one survives, and becomes the 'parent' of the succeeding generations. The process can be repeated until the artist is satisfied with the form. The final result could be thought of as an example of 'evolutionary aesthetics'. Left, above: *Nine Mutations Branch Ribs* (1991); below: *Nine Mutations* (1991). Right: *Tree of Fractal Mutations* (1991).

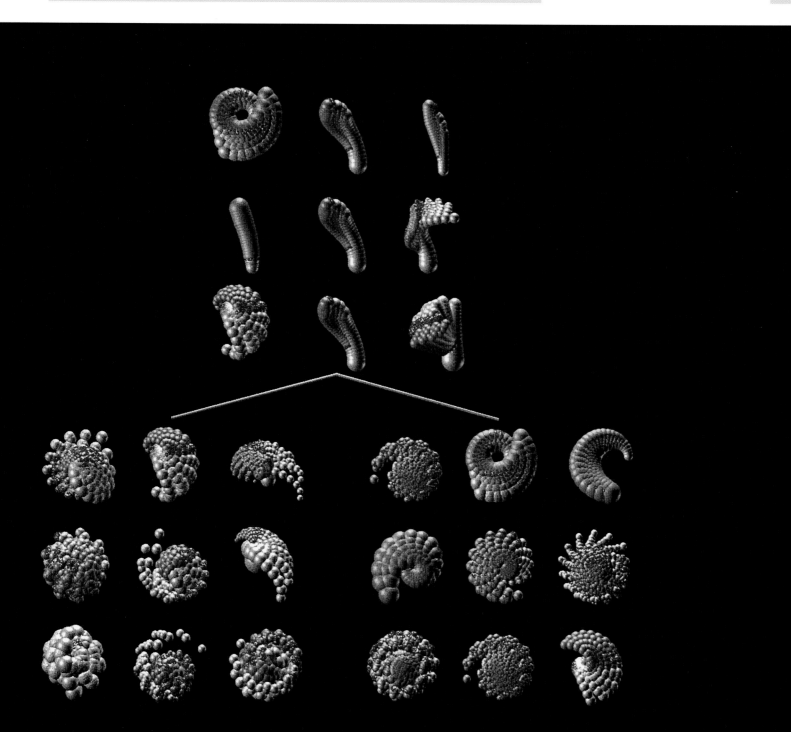

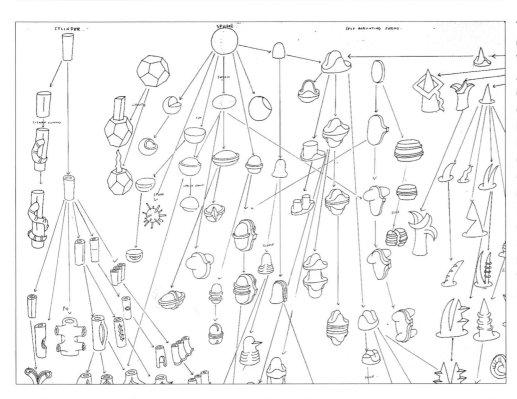

The drawing *Evolutionary Tree of Forms* (1984) shows the technique later used by William Latham with the aid of a computer. At the top of the drawing is a set of geometric primitives (cone, cube, sphere, cylinder and torus), which gradually evolve into the more complex forms near the bottom of the drawing. These forms are developed by applying a set of rules that describe sculptural transformations, such as break, stretch, bulge, scoop, twist and unite. When these transformations are carried out in a sequence, an infinite number of forms can be evolved, each slightly different from its predecessor and from its successor, though a 'family resemblance' is sustained.

Other complex problems, such as weather forecasting, economic models, social models and even armament systems, have also used genetic algorithms and neural networks in combination to study systems that involve the complex interaction of many variables.

Such software is intriguing, and it would be interesting to speculate on its possible use for the production of sculpture. In his work *Evolutionary Tree of Forms*, William Latham used a biological metaphor to develop a series of forms that shared a family resemblance. Although it used a computer to generate the forms, Latham's work was largely done 'by hand'; but some of his later work does use algorithms that allow the viewer to control the outcome. 'A detailed form is made by choosing a specific set of parameters. This can be done in various ways. The user may adjust the parameters analytically to try to achieve a particular effect. The parameters can be attached to valuator devices for user manipulation; for a complex structure this is too slow. Our preferred method is to use Mutator, which lets the user "steer" to a good form or set of forms by a series of subjective decisions.'[12]

In contrast to genetic algorithms, which are seen as being to some extent independent of the user, Latham's work is based on the need for subjective intervention in the process of form-creation. Karl Sims, a researcher and artist-in-residence at the Thinking Machines Corporation in California, takes a similar view. He intervenes by selecting which branches in the evolutionary tree should survive, and which should fade out of existence, using human judgment as the determining factor.

Applied to the area of design, such software could seek optimal solutions to a particular problem. It could become a background tool that would be able to evolve differing solutions, which could then be appraised for their relative value.

Neural Networks

The serial computer, with its ability to process data at phenomenal speeds, is now a legendary product. In just over a few decades it has provided a tool of immense power. However, there are certain built-in limitations to its performance. The very nature of serial processing means that it can only deal with one piece of information at a time. Even if each element is processed extremely quickly, it is still only a step-by-step process. This also has an effect on the type of problems that computers can solve; they are unable to deal with tasks that cannot be reduced to small, discrete parcels of information.

The development of parallelism in neural networks to some extent deals with the problems of serial processing. By taking the example of the brain and modelling it in silicon, it provides an alternative method of processing, which can deal with the fuzzy and complex issues that cannot be handled by conventional serial methods. The idea behind neural networks was derived from the way in which the neurons in the brain accomplish cognitive tasks with great rapidity, even though the individual elements work quite slowly. The brain has evolved a system whereby a vast number of nerve cells work in parallel. This is why it performs so effectively and can deal with highly complex information. It processes data against a background of learned experience, which is then stored to support future processing tasks.

The most popular neural network, the Rumelhart Net (named after its inventor David Rumelhart), combines a number of 'hidden slabs' between an input and an output surface. The net learns from being taught by examples in the form of instructions on the input surface. There the signal is translated into a series of 'connection weights', which represent its strength as it passes down the pathways from neuron to neuron. These impulses dictate how the net stores the signal; it remembers which pathways were activated and how far the signal penetrated into the hidden slabs. To see if the net has learnt from the example, a similar one is given, and the net is asked to respond in a predetermined manner, to indicate whether it recognizes the example. If the net gives the wrong answer, then it is provided with further examples. This causes it to readjust the weight connections between the neurons until the correct answer is provided. In this manner the net learns, for example, to distinguish between photographs of men and women, to judge when a subway platform is full or empty, and to recognize written or spoken language – almost impossible tasks for conventional computer systems.

Because a neural network can learn very complicated things by example and instruction, when it is turned loose on perceptual input, it can make sense of what it 'sees'. As it processes pieces of information, its internal state is altered as it adapts to variations across a whole range of examples. Eventually, a stable pattern of connections emerges, which has been built up by comparing a whole family of examples. This pattern is a representation or image of the information fed into the network.

Getting computers to 'see' has been a problem, but if predictions for neural networks are accurate, then within a few years many complex visual problems that have traditionally been a human preserve could be turned over to the computer. In conventional computing, problems where information is 'fuzzy' or incomplete have been too difficult to process. In art and design, for example, particularly in the early creative stages, traditional sketching techniques are very unfocused, as tacit knowledge is used to explore alternative ideas. In such contexts the neural network could well prove an ideal assistant.

NEW DESIGN TOOLS

Rapid Prototyping

Different computer applications have different display needs. In many applications the virtual model that appears on the computer monitor is sufficient, and is the type usually associated with computer-generated three-dimensional modelling. This type of model is ideal when form and colour are being developed interactively, as these characteristics are constantly changing during the iterative development of a design. But in the design process, plateaus are reached when certain form and colour relationships become static, and it is at these points that there arises the need for a snapshot physical model. This would mean down-loading the data and employing extensive numerically controlled machining to create a model – something that could take considerable time.

Workstations of the future will include a new function that could be represented by a button marked 'model'. Pressing this button would send details of a three-dimensional model – just created on the workstation – to a large box sitting on the floor. Currently, this box is called a rapid prototyper, a three-dimensional printer or a free-form fabricator. It produces a physical model of the design within hours, so that the designer can check the details and make whatever modifications are necessary at the desktop.

Driven by the pressures of ever-decreasing product cycle times, engineers and designers, in the US and Japan, are looking to rapid prototyping to provide the solution. It could substantially reduce the time-consuming tooling traditionally required to produce models, prototypes and parts from CAD systems. There is often the need to make a physical model of complex geometries, but such models are only ever required in very small numbers and in conventional materials. This would also remove the bottleneck that occurs between the conceptual design and the manufacturing process, by bringing the model shop to the desktop. Ultimately, it would enable the designer to produce a physical model from a virtual one, thus reasserting the role of the three-dimensional model.

Most of the rapid prototyping systems that are currently available, or in development, are based on some form of layering process. These take horizontal cross-sectional data from CAD systems and, starting with the lowest cross-section, create a layer with identical dimensions to those of the electronic cross-section. A second layer is created on top of the first and so on, with the

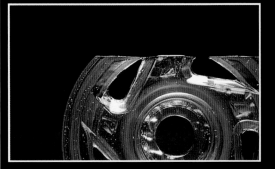

cross-sectional dimensions changing fractionally for each layer until the entire product is complete. In resin-based systems the object is then cured in an ultraviolet light oven. Although this may seem a very simple and efficient process, a number of constraints are being experienced in using these systems. However, as the technology and techniques improve many of these problems will be overcome. Main image and insets: stereo-lithography model for a car wheel.

In sterolithography, which is the most common system of rapid prototyping, the surface or solid CAD model of the object is 'sliced' horizontally. This is done electronically to produce very thin cross-sections of the object, each with its own unique profile. The information is passed to a laser, which hardens the two-dimensional profile in a vat of resin. The model is then built up in the vat, layer on layer, until the form is complete. Finally, it is removed to harden in a curing oven. Other versions employ various systems of fusion, using powder, waxes or even paper to construct laminations that are gradually built up to provide the complete form.

At present these products are more like appearance models than working prototypes, but it seems that in the future this technology could produce objects in the true material, exhibiting all the characteristics associated with it. Conceptually, rapid prototyping moves the concept of manufacturing away from a mechanical process – first begun with the Industrial Revolution – towards an entirely new form of fabrication. It allows a flexibility of operation that was impossible, or impossibly time-consuming, with conventional systems.

Digital Publications

The traditional printed page will not survive as the major instrument for the distribution of information, because it will be unable to compete effectively with the new information formats. These offer the potential for lower costs together with growing machine intelligence. By the year 2000 most organizations will be digitally based. The development of non-print media means that they will be able to communicate with still and moving images, text, graphics and audio, and use them interactively. This has been called Hyperpublishing.[13] It will affect the tools, methods and end products of publishing by redefining what is now known as electronic publishing, by transforming the publication process, and by introducing new forms of publication. As a result of these changes, authors, designers, publishers and illustrators will link up electronically to produce interactive documents that have been adapted to the personal needs and predispositions of the user.

The component technologies are in place, and prototype publications are in the final stages of development. Digital newspapers and magazines are using computerized 'agents' to browse databases and select specific news items and other articles that they have been programmed to find. This information will then be compiled into a personal newspaper or magazine, which will contain only those items that the agents were asked to seek. The result is a new kind of printing, where the selection of information is placed firmly in the hands of users. They can delegate the actual search for information to the electronic agents, telling them, for example, to scan for items on particular days, to look for all articles on computing, to collect the leader from *The Times*, or select items covering any combination of interests.

Landform Topographics uses a layer-by-layer fabrication technique to take digital colour printing into the third dimension. This process allows each layer to be coloured, gradually building up a fully coloured, three-dimensional object.

Embedded in these electronic documents will be background information in the form of computer simulations, which indicate the range and level of coverage required on a given topic. Computer animations will add to these presentations, and the user will be able to choose from a range of commentators on a given subject, ensuring a variety of views. Once the electronic document has been assembled, it could be distributed in one of the new digital formats, such as CD (Compact Disc), CD ROM (Compact Disc Read-Only Memory), CDTV (Compact Disc Television) and CD-I (Compact Disc Interactive) or other electronic media, and displayed on a domestic or commercial replay unit.

Electronic maintenance manuals are the first evidence of this approach. They will show specific tasks that the user needs to understand, and will display an interactive on-line help function. Feedback from the users will revise each new edition of the manual, thus making it more appropriate to the task in hand. The new documentation will begin to exhibit some understanding of the user and shape its information profile to that understanding.

The new publishing will consider information as a commodity that can be provided on demand and in a form that is most useful to the consumer. From the designer's standpoint, the important issue is not so much the technology involved, but the fact that the conventions for this new form of digital publication have yet to be established. This is an ideal opening for the artist and designer, who can apply their electronic design skills to the problem and provide guidelines for the look and feel of such publications.

TRANSFORMING TOMORROW 5

Much has been said about the age of information and the key role that it will play in the future of the industrialized nations. The ability of companies, including design organizations, to compete successfully will depend largely on how much information they gather, what kind of information it is, where it is positioned and how it is used. Some organizations will collect information, others will package, store and distribute it. Still others will provide products and services that allow individuals or other organizations to collect, process and distribute their own information.

Many studies[1] see the economy of the future as information-driven. Information will become a vital resource, obtaining a status similar to that of the workforce, materials and finance in the contemporary industrial scene.[2] The success of both commercial and educational enterprises will depend on how information is managed, ensuring that the right information gets to the right people at the right time, and in a form that they will find useful. The enabling technology, namely the computer, will be central to this whole process, supplying information and acting as the channel by which it is encoded into a usable form.

Richard Saul Wurman, in his extraordinary book *Information Anxiety* (1989),[3] provides a unique view of the information-overload that exists in contemporary society, by indicating just how much information – or pure data – someone living in the latter part of the twentieth century has to deal with. He says 'A weekday edition of the *New York Times* contains more information than the average person was likely to come across in a lifetime in seventeenth-century England.' One reason for this huge increase is the elaborate development of techniques for capturing data (p. 159). The camera, the video camera and now the digital camera, for example, all produce endless streams of visual data.

So long as the data was contained within a particular medium, such as the camera or the vinyl record, although the sheer volume of material made it difficult to handle, it was still possible to control. It was partly constrained by the physical storage systems themselves. Filing cabinets, drawers, cases, shelves, chests, cupboards and boxes were all modelled on items of domestic wooden furniture, which had material restrictions on size, as they had to be lifted and to fit through doorways.

Ever since the physical limitations on both the nature of the information and its storage were removed, by the computer, the 'firehoses' of information have been pumping out increasingly large amounts of data. This is at present being stored, on the assumption that at some point in the future it will be analysed. But as the means of data-capture move from an analogue to a digital format, not only is more data produced, but all data is now interchangeable. Cross-referencing is therefore increased, producing even more data. The management of this information will be impossible without a technological base. More and more businesses are using computers to manage this resource, which will be the key commodity of the future, enabling effective commercial competition.

The alternative to too much data is too little. Many organizations suffer from this form of starvation. Typically, in such cases, information needs have either been neglected or supplied on a piecemeal basis. This means that the strategic use of information cannot be exploited, as it is never possible to see the entire picture of an organization. Alternatively, considerable information may be stored in such a way – on paper, in filing cabinets and file indexes – that it is difficult to gain access to it. Nor is there any attempt to add value by cross-referencing it, so that new patterns can be extracted.

However, the information-driven economy does not just depend on whether we have too much information or too little. More important are questions of what kind of information it is, what it represents, and how the information providers are changing.

Mapping the Future

Many analysts agree that the map of the computer industry and its associated businesses will soon look very different. They suggest that there will be a convergence of traditional businesses, brought about by the need to cooperate, rather than to compete. They predict that the computer, media/publishing, consumer electronics, photographic and imaging industries, telecommunications and entertainment businesses will become closely interdependent. The technologies will overlap, and the distinctions between them will gradually disappear as the information base for these industries becomes digital.

The Centre for Information Policy Research at Harvard University has produced software that represents the interrelationships of the various information providers by mapping them on to a two-dimensional surface (see overleaf). The map has two axes; the X axis moves from products to services, and the Y axis from medium to message, or form to content. Products and services were selected for the vertical axis largely because commercial activity is currently interpreted in these terms. Medium and message, on the horizontal axis, distinguish between 'companies that provide means for recording, processing and transmitting information and those companies that traditionally have viewed themselves as producers of information, such as publishers.'[4]

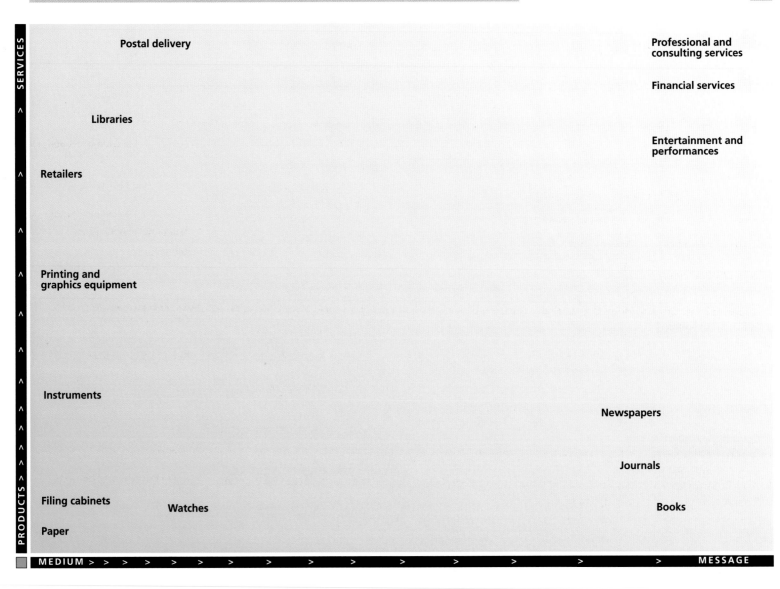

On the surface of the map a number of information entries are spatially located according to their position on each axis (see diagram p. 187). So postal services, for example, are in the top lefthand corner, with telecommunication services slightly to their right. Although they are common conveyers of information, they are to an extent concerned with content characteristics, such as duration and log-on procedures. Broadcasters are further to the right, because they provide the content of broadcasting, as well as the means of distribution, but have no physical products. Professional services, broadly located in the top right quadrant, include writers, artists and scientists, while designers and architects would be positioned further down the scale towards the product end of the axis. The results of the efforts of the professional services – books, records,

The graph above shows the basic structure of the information business map, and it forms the basis of the other maps that follow. This particular example represents the late eighteenth century. The areas of blank space represent the inventions of later centuries. The graphs that follow have been adapted slightly for the purposes of this book.

SERVICES

Postal delivery and courier services

Telephone services

Broadcasting networks
Cable networks

Professional and consulting services

Telex

Videotext

Direct broadcast satellite

On-line databases

Financial and advertising

Mobile and paging services

Teletext

Libraries

Time-sharing service bureaux

Data-processing

Mail order catalogues

Entertainment and performances

E-Mail

Teleconferencing

Retailers

PABX

Custom software

Telephone switching equipment

Modems
Mainframe computers

Workstations

Packaged software

On-line directories

Transmission equipment

Mini-computers

Market research reports

Personal computers

Directories

Printing and graphics equipment

Terminals

Autotellers

Notebook computers

Videogame consoles

Video games

Word-processors

CD and video discs
Film, TV and video

Cellular telephones

TV sets

Point of sale

Radios, video cassette recorders and stereo players

Electronic reference

Records and cassettes

Printers

Spell-checkers

Tape decks

Copiers Fax

Newspapers

Cash registers
Typewriters

Microfilm and microfiche

Newsletters

Dictation equipment

Autodiallers

Magazines and journals

Blank Magnetic media

Filing cabinets

Watches

Calculators

Books

Paper

PRODUCTS

MEDIUM > > > > > > > > > > > > > MESSAGE

paintings, buildings and objects – are in the lower half of the diagram. Newspapers are placed slightly to the left of books because of their distribution system, and in the lower left quadrant are the 'dumb' products, such as paper, typewriters and filing cabinets. As information is added to these products they tend to move towards the lower right quadrant, and as their ability to communicate with other kinds of information improves, they move even further in that direction. This indicates that the Y axis has a further dimension, which could be described as the added value of information. As the product becomes more intelligent, it moves towards the right.

The entries are all fairly common, and represent either major industry segments, individual products or services, and a few technological systems. They are included for

The information business map for the late twentieth century.

SERVICES

Postal delivery and courier services

Telephone services
Mobile and paging services

Telex

Broadcasting networks
Cable networks
Teleconferencing
Direct broadcast satellite

Data-processing
Database and videotext

Professional and consulting services

Financial and advertising

Libraries

Billing and metering services
Industrial networks

On-line databases

Teletext

Retailers

Private automatic branch exchanges

Telephone switching equipment

Time-sharing service bureaux

On-line directories

Modems

Packaged software

Custom software

Copiers
Printing and graphics equipment
Cash registers

COMPUTERS

Directories

Cellular telephones

Tape decks
Fax
Word-processors
Video tape recorders
Cameras and video cameras

Audio records and cassettes

Newspapers

Film, TV and video

Typewriters
Dictation equipment

Calculators

Newsletters

Autodiallers

Magazines and journals

Blank magnetic media
Filing cabinets

Microfilm and microfiche

Calculators

Books

Paper

PRODUCTS

MEDIUM > > > > > > > > > > > > > > MESSAGE

a variety of reasons: 'Many represent major markets, growing or shrinking in competition with surrounding entries. Others are, or will be, the subject of prolonged public disputes. A few have been added simply to illustrate the dimensions of the map and to provide checkpoints for moving from one sector to another.'[5] No mathematical or statistical methods were used for the location of the entries, as the map was constructed on the basis of perception rather than precision. The resulting pattern of distribution may not be accurate in an objective sense, therefore, but it does suggest the relationships between entries, offering insights through comparisons rather than absolutes. Sometimes the location of entries should perhaps overlap, but for the sake of clarity they have simply been placed in close proximity. This may create a sense of greater functional separation

The traditional office provides an example of the major changes that will occur in industrial and commercial life. The shaded portion covers the most general of the office activities shown on the information business map.

SERVICES

^ ^ ^ ^ ^ ^ ^ ^ ^

PRODUCTS >

Postal delivery and
courier services

Telephone services
Mobile and paging
services
Teleconferencing
Telex

Broadcasting networks
Cable networks

Data-processing
Database and
videotext

Professional and
consulting services

Direct broadcast
satellite

Financial and
advertising services

Libraries

Billing and metering
services
Industrial networks

Time-sharing service
bureaux

On-line databases

Teletext

Retailers
News stands

Telephone switching
equipment

PABXs

Custom software

On-line directories

Modems

Packaged software

Copiers
Printing and graphics
equipment
Cash registers

COMPUTERS

Audio records and
cassettes
Film, TV and video

Cellular telephones

VCRs
Tape decks
Microfilm and microfiche
Fax
Word-processors
Video tape recorders
Cameras and video cameras

Directories

Newspapers

Typewriters
Dictation equipment

Calculators

Newsletters

Autodiallers

Magazines and journals

Blank magnetic media
Filing cabinets

Microfilm and
microfiche

Books

Paper

MEDIUM > > > > > > > > > > > > > **MESSAGE**

than occurs in reality. The space between the groupings also implies separation, which is used to establish the 'spread' or coverage of the map; using the software, it is possible to 'zoom' in on any section of the map and enlarge it to obtain more detail. Some locations may then change, as more specific information provides greater precision.

The map constructed for the late eighteenth century (p. 186) gives a useful indication of the beginnings of the role of information. The invention of the telegraph, telephone and radio in the nineteenth and early twentieth centuries revolutionized the way information was distributed. The development of photography and the phonograph allowed the storage and replication of images and sound, and in the early twentieth century they were combined to create 'talking pictures'.

The introduction of the computer into the office telescopes many separate functions and transforms communication both internally and externally. Three main areas emerge: data-processing, telecommunications and office equipment; linked by the computer, these now form the basis of the electronic office of the future.

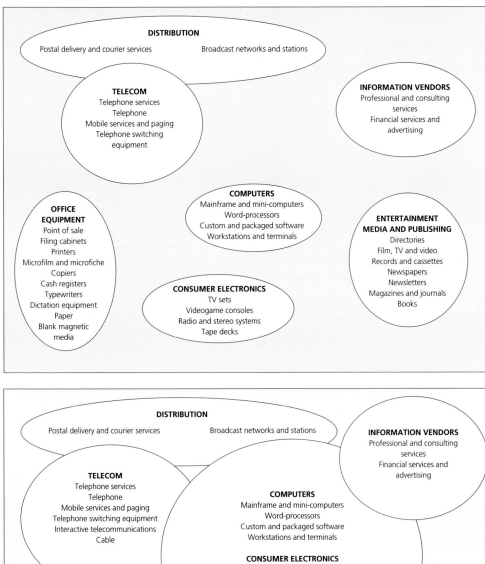

Apple computers used these mapping techniques to determine what technology might look like over a period of thirty years. In this simplified map for the 1970s the information industry reveals separate and parochial entries, with the seven sub-areas inwardly focused and mostly concerned with internal growth.

In another decade the picture looks very different. There are many overlaps between all seven sub-areas, and some, such as computers and consumer electronics, are almost completely integrated. There is the potential for many alliances to be formed between products, services, container and content, and it could be, indeed, that these labels are no longer relevant. Many new services and products are enabled by the application of computer power to enter new areas outside the traditional computer domain, such as HDTV, ISDN (international subscriber dialling networks) and interactive education and entertainment.

By that time, wires and radio waves carried signals, and experiments with television were well advanced. Although these systems were developed separately, the wires, cables and radio waves are now shared. For example, the telephone system, originally used for person-to-person contact, today carries data for computers, information for fax machines and recorded messages. The sharing of the communication technologies is not the only change that has taken place. It is now possible to choose the mode of delivery. A news item may be transmitted, ending up on the printed page, on television or displayed on a computer screen; the final decision is made, not at the outset, but only after the process of transmission.

It is the computer that has enabled this. It reduces text, sound and images to the same digital format, and thus provides the basis for convergence. Services that could once only be distributed in a single form, such as print, can now be delivered in many different ways, depending on what is most appropriate for the consumer.

This convergence, and issues of content and infrastructure in the new technologies, will have a profound effect on what designers do and how they do it. The relationship between these converged industries and the erasing of many traditional boundaries between businesses will affect the nature and extent of the electronic office. Apple computers commissioned the Harvard Centre for Information Policy Research to produce maps of the information industry for the years 1971, 1981 and 2001, to see what differences might occur and what convergences were likely. They revealed an overwhelming transformation.

The software and hardware that will enable this transformation to take place are already beginning to appear in the form of ever more powerful computers, with ever greater storage capacity, capable of carrying out millions of calculations per second. There seems no limit to the number of transistors that can be included on a chip – it could soon be one billion – and the power of today's super-computer could soon be available in the home and the office. The cables that connect one site to another will become thinner than a human hair, as fibre-optic cables become almost microscopic, fed by lasers brighter than the sun and finer than a grain of salt. Airwaves will be exploited so that real 'wireless' communication with almost infinite capacity will re-establish individual choice and provide a high level of professional service.

Directions for Design

In the design world the view of information as a commodity has yet to take firm root. This will only happen when the design culture places information on the same level of importance as its workforce and finance, and recognizes technology as the enabler. Central to all this is the need to remodel the design disciplines to absorb the new technologies, and to recognize that the sharing of information creates new alignments. This will mean a move from the one-to-one correspondences of the old tools to the matrix of interrelationships that forms the basis of the new electronic design office.

For this to become a reality, the design organizations must view computing not just as a technical tool limited to certain areas of design, but as the strategic business environment of the future. Predictions centre on the development of a global industry, providing new products and services as a result of the convergence of traditional businesses. What will the effect be on the design community? How will it fit into this picture, and what will be the nature of the new design activity?

The electronic revolution is likely to bring as much change to working practices as the Industrial Revolution before it. The Industrial Revolution can be seen as technology-driven;

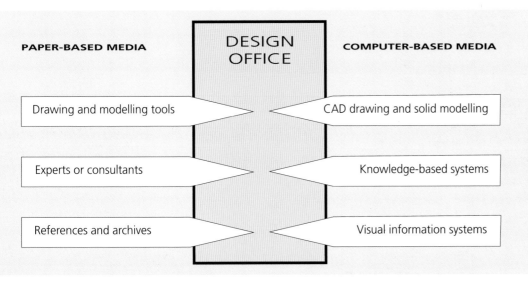

PAPER-BASED MEDIA

DESIGN OFFICE

COMPUTER-BASED MEDIA

Drawing and modelling tools — CAD drawing and solid modelling

Experts or consultants — Knowledge-based systems

References and archives — Visual information systems

This diagram shows a transcription from traditional processes to electronic ones. At the moment there is a one-to-one substitution of familiar skills, but the future picture could be far more complex.

the powered spinning machine and the steam engine were major triggers in the growth of the factory system, which was to typify the industrialization of Europe and the United States. The resulting working methods, which led to the de-skilling of the workforce, are part of the inheritance still found in the office and the factory.

The new electronic technologies could begin to allow workers much more control over their time and place of work. Certainly, architect Walter Kleeman insists, the location of the office will no longer need to be fixed, as it is today: 'the office is a *place* where an employee must be between specified *times* to suffer a variety of interruptions ... tomorrow an office will be a *system*, accessible via the terminal from *any place at any time*.'[6]

The car and train have become recent extensions of the office, with the mobile phone and laptop computer allowing many traditionally office-based tasks to be undertaken while travelling at speed. This applies equally to aeroplanes, another realistic alternative to the office, as sky-phones and other forms of sophisticated communication equipment installed in aircraft allow business travellers to continue the office routine at a height of 45,000 feet.

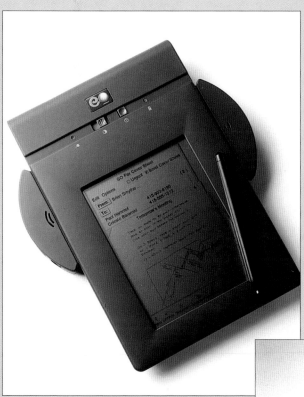

Looking at the role of the computer in products for the next decade is a process that requires a great deal of imagination, but it is not an impossible task for designers. In the near future there is the Personal Digital Assistant (PDA) from Apple, which takes the form of a pen-based palm computer called Newton. Combining communication and computing, the object resembles a pocket notebook rather than a conventional computer. As these products become smaller and more powerful, the computer 'feel' disappears, allowing them to be fully integrated into daily life. The notebook device from EO Europe is similar in character. It has been described as an 'out-of-box' experience, because the machine can be unpacked and in use within fifteen minutes, with no need for the user to learn anything new.

Over the next decade the computer will move away from the traditional object as we know it today, with its screen, keyboard and mouse, until it becomes virtually indistinguishable from the products that contain it. Examples of near future products are Orbitor, an interactive globe system, Aviator, an interface to a computer database, the electronic information-finder, the music workstation and the traveller's guide, Terravellar. This is the kind of integration that is expected as consumer electronics and the computer converge.

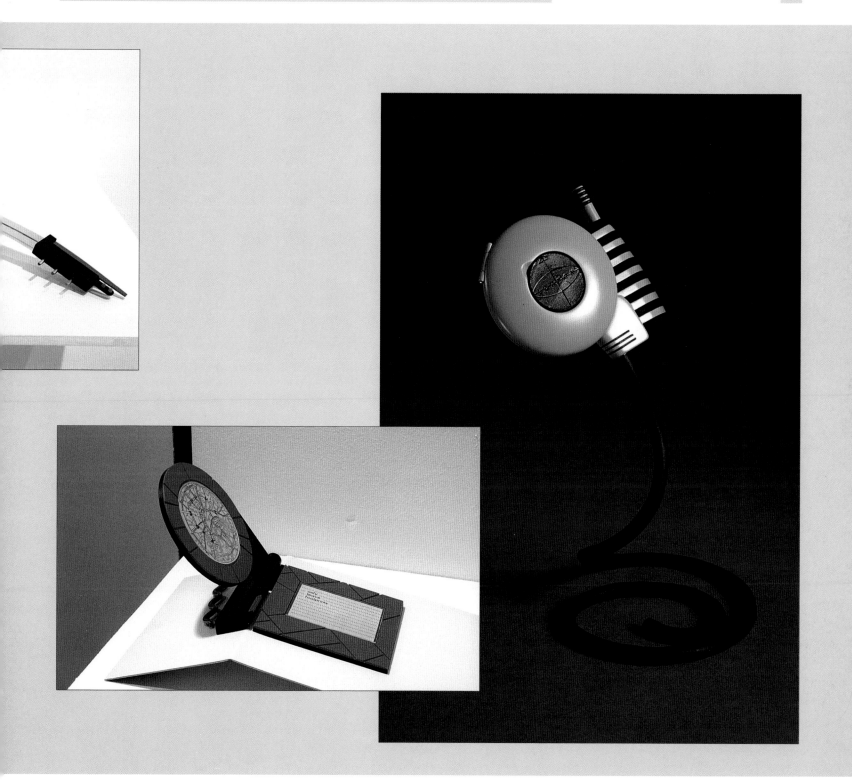

Xerox has spent considerable time and money looking at the 'office without walls', where communication is conducted via video-phones; the office becomes a virtual space, reducing the limitations of distance. Video-conferencing is an extension of this, and the prediction of the 'electronic cottage' could become a reality once cable and satellite connections become more commonplace. Virtual reality and high levels of computer simulation, such as tele-presencing, are another electronic attempt to cancel the legacy of the Industrial Revolution.

As the limitations of time and place are removed from the traditional workplace, the design office must follow this trend towards dispensing with conventions. In the short term, a number of technological changes will form the new design arena and indicate how it will look in the transitional period, before the medium of computing is fully exploited.

It is probable that the separate kinds of information now handled by designers, often in a linear sequence, will begin to combine, so that words, sound, still and moving images, two-dimensional drawings and three-dimensional models will be processed in parallel. The designer will work in the 'foreground' on any one of these aspects, while the others are updated by the computer in the 'background'. Sound notes could accompany drawings to explain aspects of an idea, and video clips could provide contextual background information to the project. Access to databases of information will be commonplace, and images will be 'intelligently' updated with cost and production information, so that the implications of a design decision can be examined at a much earlier stage in the process. An electronic 'scrapbook', containing images, text and sound, could be created as the designer uses the new technologies to collect relevant examples from the wealth of visual and verbal information around them, which designers 'read' so effectively. As these scrapbooks become large and unmanageable, 'agents' could be instructed to make selections for the designer, and to produce material that could be used for the project. They could also provide historical examples of other objects, projects or designs that might be incorporated into the current work.

Computer games are also expected to move away from the small screen and hand-held joystick towards a more participative mode of interaction.

Methods of interacting with the computer system will diversify and proliferate; they will no longer be restricted to the traditional keyboard – the only option available to most current computer users. Gloves, helmets, lenses and other items of clothing will become commonplace, providing more intuitive ways of handling three-dimensional models. When natural interfaces have become more robust, talking, writing and gesturing to the computer will cancel the need for the more visual interfaces that are used today.

The processing power of the machine will be sufficient to produce interactively real-time, ray-traced and radiosity (p. 79) images, so that colour-accurate, photorealistic images will be available during the design process. Design details will be taken care of as part of the network facility; a user will be able to look up approved technical soloutions and incorporate them into the work, either as they appear, or modified to suit a particular circumstance. The high-level services provided by the network could include advice and assistance on mechanical aspects of a design, stress analysis and structural issues. In addition, they might include many computationally intensive functions that are at present separate.

The more or less standard interface that designers have to deal with today will disappear. A limiting factor of many systems is the problem of having to handle the same information, irrespective of either the ability of the user or the nature of the design task. In the future, users will be able to represent a wide diversity of functional capabilities typically used in the design, manufacturing and organizational sectors of the profession.

Teams of designers will be able to develop interactive scenarios for a project, sharing information and ideas without being in the same space or time zone. These developments in work practices, which look towards the future of the electronic design studio, are already beginning to appear in current methods of design. There is no doubt that the design studio is in a period of transition, as both technological and organizational pressure builds to encourage and drive the change. The introduction of computer systems and the conversion to a digital base has allowed the gradual development of skill and expertise in the design community that seeks to displace earlier methodologies.

Such a move was first seen in a few pioneering studios of the 1970s. Dedicated and committed practices, usually in architecture, installed very expensive and cumbersome equipment; they were prepared to pick up the high costs and other risks involved to be first in the field. These practices, worldwide, could probably be numbered on the fingers of two hands. Although small in number, however, they were responsible for initiating a change in the culture that was to lead, some time later, to a greater acceptance of computer systems by the design profession.

This is how the situation appears today. Increasing numbers of design studios are being equipped with computer systems. Application software has been well tried and tested, particularly the monochrome computer systems that provided a platform for the launch of the desktop-publishing revolution. There were three components that convinced designers that the technology was worth the investment: the affordable personal computer, page-description formats such as Postscript (p. 86), and reliable and relatively high-resolution laser printers. Designers were reassured to find that their existing skills could be translated directly into the computer, so that many of their existing work practices need not be changed substantially. Start-up costs are now very low, and a strong competitive advantage can be demonstrated for almost any installed computer base.

It is estimated[7] that the penetration of computer systems into the design studio, for use in creative work, is at present around 35 per cent. Future scenarios show an accelerated demand and a massive level of acceptance, with most offices moving into the electronic studio. While the number of installed systems remains small, the vast majority of offices can afford to ignore them. But once a critical mass has evolved, an estimated 75 to 80 per cent of studios will be forced to adopt computer systems for creative use.

The new, electronic-based designer will need tools that develop conceptual, as well as practical skills. There is a need for extensive, long-term investment in the effort to change designers' perceptions, so they can deal with the functional and cultural complexities of the new age. There are major implications for the education systems of design, which will have to strive to produce the new curricula, the new faculty, so that the new student can become the new designer.

Conclusion

In the early days, arguments for the use of computing were all about productivity gains and increased efficiency. By now the arguments have become more sophisticated. They centre around issues of usability and improvements in the quality and value of the work produced.

In the design world, the introduction of computers has certainly led to an overall raising of standards, and to a conceptual flexibility that would never have been possible with traditional media. The case for computers in art and design has already been made. But the role of the artist and designer is still evolving, and new forms of art and design work are still emerging, making this a most interesting time. How these aspects will develop is an open question.

And the responsibility for their development must lie with artists and designers. If they decline to become involved, they will forfeit any say in the tools, media and disciplines that will inevitably form the basis of most work in the twenty-first century. Exploring new uses for the medium of computing, experimenting with new techniques, providing genuinely new solutions to new problems, and – above all – humanizing the technology: these are all roles for the designer and the artist, not the technologist.

Yet this is a cause that is too important to be fought alone. We must confront it not as individuals, but as a team. It is only by combining our abilities and exploiting our contrasting outlooks that we can discover fresh visions for the technological future.

NOTES

INTRODUCTION

1 Margaret A. Boden, *The Creative Mind*, Weidenfeld and Nicolson, London, 1990
2 Joseph Weizenbaum, *Computer Power and Human Reason: From Judgment to Calculation*, Pelican Books, Harmondsworth, 1976

CHAPTER 1: COMPUTER SCIENCE, COMPUTER ART

1 C.P. Snow, Rede Lecture, 'The Two Cultures and the Scientific Revolution', 1959
2 Nigel Cross, *Design Education Research Note: Design Discipline*, Faculty of Technology, The Open University, Milton Keynes, 1982
3 Gerhard Schmitt, 'Classes of Design – Classes of Tools', in *The Electronic Design Studio: Architectural Knowledge and Media in the Computer Era*, Malcom McCullough, William Mitchell and Patrick Purcell, MIT Press, Cambridge, MA, 1990
4 Jasia Reichardt, *Studio International* special issue on 'Cybernetic Serendipity – The Computer and the Arts', London, 1968
5 *ibid*
6 *ibid*
7 Nancy Bartels, 'Artist on the Edge', in *California Confetti: Bits and Pieces for Creative Communicators*, June 1990
8 Pamela McCorduck, *Aaron's Code: Meta-Art, Artificial Intelligence and the Work of Harold Cohen*, W.H. Freeman and Co., New York, 1990
9 *ibid*

CHAPTER 2: OLD TOOLS – NEW TOOLS

1 Alan Pipes, *Drawing for Three-Dimensional Design*, Thames and Hudson, London, 1990
2 Joseph Weizenbaum, *op. cit.*
3 Joseph Weizenbaum, *op. cit.*
4 *ibid*
5 Christopher Lorenz, *The Design Dimension, Product Strategy and the Challenge of Global Marketing*, Oxford, 1986
6 Donald Michie and Rory Johnson, *The Creative Computer: Machine Intelligence and Human Knowledge*, Penguin, Harmondsworth, 1984
7 Joseph Weizenbaum, *op. cit.*
8 Herbert Franke, *Computer Graphics, Computer Art*, Phaidon, London, 1971
9 Jasia Reichardt, *The Computer in Art*, Studio Vista, London, 1971
10 Kerry Downes, *Sir Christopher Wren: The Making of St Paul's*, exhibition catalogue, Royal Academy of Arts, London, 1991

11 Rudolf Arnheim, *The Power of the Centre. A Study of Composition in the Visual Arts*, University of California Press, Berkeley, 1982
12 Ivan Sutherland, 'Sketchpad – A Man Machine Graphical Communication System', PhD thesis, MIT, Cambridge, MA, 1963
13 Shoshana Zuboff, *In the Age of the Smart Machine. The Future of Work and Power*, Heinemann, London, 1988

CHAPTER 3: TRANSFORMING THE PRESENT

1 Rick Poynor, in *Typography Now*, Booth Clibbon Editions, London, 1992
2 Max Kinsman, in *Typography Now*, *op. cit.*
3 Clement Mok, opening address to SIGGRAPH conference in Las Vegas, Nevada, 1991
4 William Leith, 'At Home with Mr Hockney', *The Independent*, 21 October 1990
5 Barbara Robertson, 'Painting in 3D', in *Computer Graphics World*, October 1991
6 Stephen Todd, William Latham and Peter Hughes, 'Computer Sculpture, Design and Animation', in *Journal of Visualization and Computer Animation*, vol. 2, 1991
7 Barbara Robertson, 'Roll over Rodin', in *Computer Graphics World*, March 1992

CHAPTER 4: TRANSFORMING REALITY

1 Frank Hayes and Nick Baran, 'A Guide to GUIs', in *BYTE*, McGraw-Hill, Hightstown, NJ, July 1989
2 *ibid*
3 Maureen Caudill, 'Kinder, Gentler Computing', in *BYTE*, April 1992
4 Laurin Herr, 'Volume Visualization', *SIGGRAPH '89 Show Daily*, 1989
5 Vannevar Bush, 'As we may think', *Atlantic Monthly*, no. 176, July 1945
6 Max Whitby, 'In Anticipation', in *Technologies for the 21st Century: On Multimedia*, Martin Greenberger (ed.), The Voyager Company, Santa Monica, CA, 1990
7 Kristina Hooper Woolsey, 'Multimedia Scouting', *IEEE Computer Graphics Applications*, IEEE Computer Society, London, July 1991
8 'Developing Multimedia Applications', *IEEE Computer Graphics Applications*, July 1991
9 John Sculley, 'Making it Happen', in *Technologies for the 21st Century: On Multimedia*, *op. cit.*
10 John Samson, 'Starting with the Human End Instead', *Computing*, 1 February 1990

11 Suran Goonatilake, 'Cracking the Code on Model Parameters', *Computing*, 28 February 1991

12 Stephen Todd, William Latham and Peter Hughes, *op. cit.*

13 'Davis Review: Hypermedia and Artificial Intelligence', in *Electronic Publishing*, vol. 1, no. 3, Davis Inc., May/June 1988

CHAPTER 5: TRANSFORMING TOMORROW

1 John McLaughlin and Anne Louise Antonoff, *Mapping the Information Business: Program on Information Resources Policy*, Centre for Information Policy Research, Harvard University, Cambridge, MA, 1986

2 Beat Hochstrasser and Catherine Griffiths, *Regaining Control of IT Investment,* Kobler Unit: Imperial College of Science and Technology, London, 1990

3 Richard Saul Wurman, *Information Anxiety*, Pan Books, London, 1989

4 John McLaughlin and Anne Louise Antonoff, *op. cit.*

5 *ibid*

6 Walter Kleeman, *Interior Design of the Electronic Office: The Comfort and Productivity Payoff*, chapter 5, 1991

7 'Davis Review: Electronic Design and Communication Arts', in *Electronic Publishing*, vol. 2, no. 1, June 1989

SURVEY OF USEFUL SOURCES

There is a very large number of exhibitions, conferences, magazines and journals that are either about computing or contain major items on computing. It would be pointless to attempt to cover such a broad field, so I have listed what I consider to be the major media events. I have personal experience of them all and can therefore recommend them as important, should you wish to keep up with this fast-moving field. I know that there are many others not mentioned here, and I apologize to those journals and organizations who feel that they should have been included.

MAGAZINES

Ars Electronica, Prix Ars Electronica
ORF, Franckstrasse 2a, A–4010 Linz, Austria
Tel: 0732 53481 267
Fax: 0732 53481 250

BYTE (UK)
McGraw-Hill Information Services
McGraw-Hill House, Shoppenhangers Road
Maidenhead, Berkshire, SL6 2QL, UK

BYTE (USA)
Byte Subscriptions
PO Box 552, Hightstown, NJ 08520, USA

Computer Graphics World
1 Technology Park Drive, PO Box 987
Westford, MA 01886, USA

Mondo 2000
PO Box 10171, Berkeley, CA 94709, USA

The Whole Earth Review
PO Box 38, Sausalito, CA 94966, USA

Wired
PO Box 191826, San Francisco, CA 94119–1826, USA

CONFERENCES AND EXHIBITIONS

Imagina
BP 300, MC9000 Monte Carlo
Tel: (33) 93 15 93 94
Fax: (33) 93 15 93 95

National Computer Graphics Association (NCGA)
2722 Merrilee Drive, Suite 200, Fairfax, VA 22031, USA
Tel: 703 698 9600

Nicograph
Ikebukuro Sunshine City
Yurakucho, Mullion, Tokyo, Japan

SIGGRAPH Conference Management
401 N Michigan Avenue, Chicago, IL 60611, USA
Tel: 312 644 6610
Fax: 312 321 6867

Technology Entertainment Design (TED)
TED Conferences Inc.
59 Wooster St, New York, NY 10012, USA
Tel: 212 219 8993
Fax: 212 219 0583

ILLUSTRATION CREDITS

The following abbreviations have been used:
a above, *b* below, *c* centre, *l* left, *r* right.

1 *Mathematica, Wolfram Research*
2–3 Correlation among spacecraft and ground observations during a polar substorm. © 1992 *Lloyd A. Treinish, IBM Thomas J. Watson Research Center*
5c © 1991 *Helmann and Hesselink, Stanford University*
5bl Microsoft Windows GUI. *Courtesy Microsoft Corporation, USA*
5br *Wolfram Research, Silicon Graphics*
6cl © 1991 *Vincent Argiro, Vital Images Inc.*
6br *SGI/IRIS, Indigo*

INTRODUCTION

8b Malcom Cox, textile design. *Royal College of Art, London (RCA)*
8–9 Interior visualization for the Mappin Terraces, London Zoo. *Catherine Rey, GMW Architects, London*
9al Film still from *The Lawnmower Man. Courtesy of Xaos Inc.*
9br William Fetter drawing. *Courtesy Boeing Aircraft Corporation*
10 The Evans & Sutherland Conceptual Design and Rendering System (CDRS) in use at the Royal College of Art. *RCA, London*
11 Exterior visualization of a hotel complex. *GMW Architects, London*

CHAPTER 1: COMPUTER SCIENCE, COMPUTER ART

12–3 IBM 360, model 65. *Courtesy IBM UK Ltd*
14c Clive Richards, *Spinning Gazebo*, 1970. *Computer Picture Book: Lanchester Polytechnic*
14cr Close-up individual icons. *Courtesy AT&T archives*
15al Leon Harmon and Kenneth Knowlton, *Studies in Perception II: Gulls*, 1968. *Courtesy AT&T archives*
15bl Manfred Mohr, drawing, 1977. *Courtesy of the artist*
15cr Ivan Sutherland using Sketchpad, 1962. *Reprinted with permission of Lincoln Laboratories, Lexington MIT, MA*
16l Alto computer, 1980. *Reprinted with permission of Xerox Corporation*
16r Macintosh II computer. *Courtesy Apple Computer UK Ltd*
17 HP ME10 software. *Courtesy Hewlett Packard*
18al Apple Graphical User Interface. *Courtesy Apple Computer UK Ltd*
18ar Windows Graphical User Interface. *Courtesy Microsoft Corporation, USA*
18cr X Windows Graphical User Interface. Courtesy *MIT, Cambridge, MA*
18br Apple mouse. *Courtesy Apple Computer UK Ltd*
19l VR flight helmet. *Courtesy Virtual Research, CA*
19ar Dexterous HandMaster. *Courtesy Exos Inc., MA*
19br Go Computer. *Courtesy Go Corporation, CA*
20 Microstation software. *Courtesy Intergraph Corporation*
21 Chapel of Notre-Dame-de-Haut, Ronchamp. *Courtesy Form Z*
22c Frieder Nake, *Klee No. 2*, 1965. From the exhibition 'Cybernetic Serendipity – The Computer and the Arts', ICA, London, October 1968
22br *Computer Graphic*, 1966. From the exhibition 'Cybernetic Serendipity – The Computer and the Arts', ICA, London, October 1968
23 Richard Hamilton, *Five Tyres Abandoned*, 1964, and *Five Tyres Remoulded*, 1971. *Courtesy of the artist*
24–5 Jeremy Gardiner, *Nature Morte*, 1990. *Courtesy of the artist*
26–7 Joan Truckenbrod, *Refraction Explosion*, 1991. *Courtesy of the artist*
27ar Karen Guzak, *Jewels for Taj*, 1990. *Courtesy of the artist*
29 Jeffrey Shaw, *Legible City*, 1989–90. *Courtesy of the artist*

CHAPTER 2: OLD TOOLS – NEW TOOLS

30 Sketch drawing. *Courtesy of the RCA, London*
31l Suzanne Smeeth, presentation drawing: Uppercut Boxing Club. *Courtesy RCA, London*
31r Tony Collett, technical drawing: elevations of library and hostel. *Courtesy RCA, London*
32 Print of early perspective drawing system. *Optics: Painting and Photography*, M.H. Pirenne, Cambridge University Press
33 Hans Holbein, *The Ambassadors*, 1533. *Courtesy National Gallery, London*
36–7 William Fetter manikin drawings. *Courtesy Boeing Aircraft Corporation*
37 Automobile CAD. *Courtesy of Alias Research, Canada*
38 Microprocessor chip from Zilog. VLSI Technology Inc. *Courtesy Computer Museum, Boston, MA*
39 Patrick Whitney, Professor and Director of the Institute of Design, Illinois Institute of Technology. Diagram showing the nine steps in the design process. From the *Design Processes Newsletter*, vol. 2, no. 3, 1988
41 Computer paint system. *Courtesy Quantel Ltd*
42–3 Stephen Pochin, *Dumping Core No. 3, Cottonmouth Construct*, 1992. *Courtesy of the artist*
43r Computer paint system. *Courtesy of Avid Technologies*
44–5 Colette and Charles Bangert, computer line drawing, 1977. *Studio*

International special issue on 'Cybernetic Serendipity – The Computer and the Arts', Jasia Reichardt, London, 1968

45ar Computer Technique Group from Japan, *Return to a Square. Studio International* special issue on 'Cybernetic Serendipity – The Computer and the Arts', Jasia Reichardt, London, 1968

45br DJ DiLeonardo, isometric view of neuron distribution. *Studio International* special issue on 'Cybernetic Serendipity – The Computer and the Arts', Jasia Reichardt, London, 1968

46 Efraim Arazi, *Transformation of a Relief Surface. Studio International* special issue on 'Cybernetic Serendipity – The Computer and the Arts', Jasia Reichardt, London, 1968

47 Leon Harmon and Kenneth Knowlton, mural, 1966. *Studio International* special issue on 'Cybernetic Serendipity – The Computer and the Arts', Jasia Reichardt, London, 1968

48 William Clere, after Sir Christopher Wren, the 'Great Model', 1674. *The Dean and Chapter of St Paul's Cathedral, London*

49al Wireframe drawing, industrial design. *Courtesy RCA, London*

49c Hidden-line removed image. *Courtesy Applicon CAD/CAM system*

49br Photorealistic rendering. *Courtesy Intergraph Corporation*

50l Architectural model. *Courtesy NHK TV*

50r Pair of eyeglasses designed with the Conceptual Design and Rendering System (CDRS). *Courtesy Evans & Sutherland*

51 Car design using the CDRS system. *Courtesy Evans & Sutherland*

51al Takako Tomiha, dressmaking simulation. *Toray Industries Inc., Research Institute for Polymers and Textiles, Japan*

53 Three cards from the Hypercard stack of designers. *Courtesy Design Museum, London*

54 Portrait of J.M. Jacquard. *Courtesy Science Museum, London*

55 Cash till and computer for use at point of sale. *Courtesy IBM UK Ltd*

CHAPTER 3: TRANSFORMING THE PRESENT

56–7 Film still from *The Empire Strikes Back*, 1977. *Industrial Light and Magic for 20th Century Fox 1977* ©

58al Typical mouse. *Courtesy Microsoft Corporation, USA*

58cr Portable, pen-based computer called 'Gridpad'. *Courtesy GRID System Corporation, USA*

Industrial Design

59a Three-dimensional wireframe computer model. *Courtesy CAD/CAM Division, Schlumberger, USA*

59bl Computer-based technical drawing. *Courtesy RCA, London, Industrial Design*

60l Teapot design. © 1989 *Spencer W. Thomas, SIGGRAPH*

60c Teapot design. © 1989 *John Prusinski, Cybergrafix, SIGGRAPH*

60r Teapot design. ©1989 *Wayne Hoit, Automated Images, SIGGRAPH*

61l Teapot design. ©1989 *Jeffrey A. Thingvold, University of Utah, SIGGRAPH*

61c Teapot design. ©1989 *Stephenson Moore Computer Graphics, SIGGRAPH*

61 Shingo Kita, Vanity Visions TV/Mirror. *Courtesy RCA, London, Industrial Design*

62–3 Three-dimensional model of an earring. *Dru Harvey, RCA, London*

64l Christian Batchelor, soft model of a video still camera: top, demonstration of the controls; centre, simulated electronic display; bottom, simulated view through the viewfinder. *Courtesy RCA, London, Computer-related Design*

64–5 Three-dimensional computer model of a hi-fi unit. *Alias Research, Canada*

66 Paul Leighton, three-dimensional computer model of a sun watch. *Courtesy Texas Instruments, USA*

67al Plastic mould simulation showing pressure variations for different injection time steps. *Courtesy SDRC*

67bl Visualization of flow fronts as a plastic mould is being filled. *Courtesy SDRC*

67ar Design for a nautical navigator. *IDEO, USA*

67cr Screen design for the Trimble NavGraphic. *IDEO, USA*

Automobile Design

68 Malcolm Ward, traditional sketch of a car design. *Courtesy RCA, London, Vehicle Design*

69bl Computer-generated concept for a car design displaying highlights. *Alias Research, Canada*

69ar Traditional model-making techniques for car design. *Courtesy RCA, London, Vehicle Design*

70–1 The Evans & Sutherland CDRS system. *Courtesy Evans & Sutherland*

72al Full-size mock-up of a car design directly machined from CDRS database. *Courtesy RCA, London, Vehicle Design*

72–3 Ray-traced image of a car in a showroom with reflected highlights. *Alias Research, Canada*

73ar The Evans & Sutherland CDRS system in use at the Royal College of Art. *Courtesy RCA, London, Vehicle Design*

Architecture and Interior Design

74–5 Ray-traced image using Swivel 3D software. *Paracomp Inc.*

76–7 Architectural rendering of BCE Place office interior. © 1991 *Design Vision Inc.*

78–9 View of the auditorium of the Candlestick Theatre. *Radiosity software by Daniel R. Baum, Steve Mann, Kevin P. Smith and James W. Winget, all of Silicon Graphics. Hardware, Silicon Graphics IRIS 4D 310 GTX. Candlestick Theatre architect, Mark Mack. Database modelling by Charles Ehrlich, Department of Architecture, University of California, Berkeley, CA*

78bl Brook's House living room, North Carolina. *Radiosity software by Daniel R. Baum, Steve Mann, Kevin P. Smith and James W. Winget, all of Silicon Graphics. Hardware, Silicon Graphics IRIS 4D 310 GTX. Building model copyright, the University of North Carolina, Chapel Hill*

79r Architectural rendering. *Loft Design*

80al Interior of a basilica. *Created by Osama Hashem, Osama Ltd, New York, using Wavefront's Advanced Visualizer*

80ar Interior of Le Corbusier's Ronchamp chapel, France. *Modelled by*

Keith Howie, Paul Boudreau and Eric Hanies at 3D/Eye Inc., for Hewlett Packard

80br Interior of Chartres cathedral. *Modelled by John Lin and rendered by John Wallace on an HP Apollo series 900 workstation*

81 John Nichols, interior perspective, silkscreen print. *Eisenman Architects, University of Cincinnati, College of Design and Architecture*

81r Boiler room. *Modelled by John Lin and John Wallace at 3D/Eye Inc., for Hewlett Packard*

82–3 Interior of the Mappin Terraces, London Zoo, modelled by Catherine Rey. *GMW Architects, London*

84bl Imaginary architectural interior. *Alias Research, Canada*

84–5 Imaginary architectural interior. *Raydream*

86al Exterior architectural visualization: 'the building as sign'. *Landor Associates, San Francisco*

86cl Interior architectural visualization for a London Underground station. *GMW Architects, London*

87 Exterior architectural visualization of the facade of a building at night. *GMW Architects, London*

87al Computer-aided design software used as a tool for facilities management of a building. *Intergraph Corporation*

Graphic Design

88 Page layout using desktop-publishing software. *Courtesy RCA, London, Graphic Design*

89 Poster design for *Design Quarterly*. *April Greiman*

90–1 Poster collage for *Design Quarterly*. *April Greiman*

91bl *Architecture: Education and Instruction*, poster collage for *Design Quarterly*. *April Greiman*

91br Textile design. *Polyester Institute of Japan*

92al Poster design for the Walker Art Museum's exhibition 'Graphic Design in America', 1989–90. *April Greiman*

92bc Poster, '24-hour Turnaround'. *Mark Anderson Design*

92cr 'An Exercise in Utilities'. *MacWorld Magazine*

93al Poster for a Computer-Related Design Course at the RCA, London. *Whynot boys, London*

93cr Textile design. *Harlequin fabric, upholstery for the Cerritos Centre for the Performing Arts*

93bc 'The New Discourse: Cranbrook Design 1980–1990'. *Cranbrook Design Studio*

94 Rough layouts faxed to clients. *April Greiman: Bellini office furniture*

94–5 Random typefaces. *Erik van Blokland and Just van Rossum, Font Works*

95c Constructing type in a computer. *Courtesy RCA, London, Graphic Design*

96–7 Stephen Pochin, *Dumping Core No. 1, Medici Hinterwelt*, 1992. *Courtesy of the artist*

Textile and Fashion Design

98bl Nested pattern blocks. *Lectra Systems*

98cr Gerber Creative Designer system. *Gerber Technologies*

99al Man's jacket design constructed using the Rapid Response

Computer system. *Computer Design, Inc.*

99ar Pattern block for a sleeve. *Courtesy RCA, London*

99bl Skirt design, using the Rapid Response Computer system. *Computer Design, Inc.*

99br Jacket design, using the Rapid Response Computer system. *Computer Design, Inc.*

100ar Texture-wrapped images. *Computer Design, Inc.*

100b RCA fashion/textile research project. *Courtesy RCA, London*

101 Texture-wrapped models. *Computer Design, Inc.*

102–3 Malcom Cox, textile designs. *Courtesy RCA, London*

Photography

104–5 Quantel Paintbox-retouched image for Malvern Star, by the Campaign Palace. *Courtesy Quantel*

105 Mike Valente, 'No Way', Mamba-retouched image for BMW. *Crosfields Electronics*

106 Morey Fish commercial. *Courtesy Barco Graphics, UK*

107 Paul Biddle, 'Fish', Mamba-retouched image. *Crosfields Electronics*

108–9 Monmartre Visuals. *Courtesy Barco Graphics, UK*

110l David Hockney, still video composite portrait of Colin Ford, No. 1, 29 August 1990. *Courtesy of the artist*

110r David Hockney, still video composite portrait of Lisa McPherson, 6 September 1990. *Courtesy of the artist*

Design Crafts

112al Design for a ring on the Intergraph computer system, and photograph of the ring when made. *Stewart Devlin*

112ac Three views of a computer-modelled ring design. *Stewart Devlin*

112cr Design for a piece of jewelry made by stereolithography. *Courtesy 3D Systems*

112bl Design for a silver pomander. *Rebecca de Quin*

112br Design for a piece of jewelry. *Tony Pack*

113a Peter Stuck, model of a coffee pot handle, and rendered model of the complete coffee pot, using Alias software. *David Queensbury Associates*

113c Experimental ceramics. *John Lewell: Computer Graphics Orbis, London, 1985*

113br Ceramic forms generated by the 'Knowledge from Beauty' software. *Paul Adelson and Terry Franguiadakis, School of Art and Design, University of Chicago*

Film and Animation

114 Film still from *Alien*. *System Simulation for 20th Century Fox*

115 Still from a *Snowman* animation. *Pixar*

116 Matt Elson, polygonal surface drawing of Lotta Desire. *Symbolics, Inc.*

117 Matt Elson, Lotta Desire in *Virtually Yours*, 1989. *Symbolics Inc.*

118c Film still from *The Abyss*. *20th Century Fox 1989 ©*

118bl *The Abyss*. *Industrial Light & Magic for 20th Century Fox 1989 ©*

118–9 Transformation of a face into an abstract design. *Dru Harvey, RCA, London*

120l Frame from the film *Flashback* with a simulated Marilyn Monroe. *Directors Nadia M. Thalmann and Daniel Thalmann. Numerical software Benoit Lafleur, Computer Graphics Lab., Swiss Federal Institute of Technology and MIRA Lab., University of Geneva* ©
120r Frame from the film *Still Walking* with a simulated Marilyn Monroe. *Directors Nadia M. Thalmann and Daniel Thalmann. Design Arghyro Paouri. Walking software Ronan Boulic, Computer Graphics Lab., Swiss Federal Institute of Technology and MIRA Lab., University of Geneva* ©
121 Silver Suzy. *Mr Film, CA*
122l *The Lawnmower Man*, 1992. *Courtesy Xaos Inc.*
122–3 *Terminator 2. Industrial Light and Magic for Tri Star Pictures* ©

Painting
125 Blell, *The Circus Animals' Desertion and Saltimbanques*, 1988–9. *Courtesy of the artist*
126al Paint system menu. *Time Arts Inc., Oasis software*
126b Software palette. *Time Arts Inc., Oasis software*
127ac Watercolour technique. *AXA Corporation, Oasis software*
127cl Gouache technique. *Time Arts Inc., Oasis software*
127bc Watercolour technique. *Time Arts Inc., Oasis software*
128bl Char Davies, *Pebble*, 3D still image created interactively using animation software, Softimage, 1992
128–9 Char Davies, *Root*, 3D still image using Softimage software, 1992
130al Harold Cohen, *Eden* series. *Harold Cohen*
130c Harold Cohen, *An Imagined Paradise. Harold Cohen*
130–1 Max Davies, computer-generated print, 1991. *Courtesy RCA, London*
132–3 Kenneth Snelson, *Forest Devils' Moon Night*, 1990. *Courtesy of the artist*
134a Tsuyoshi Yamamoto, algorithmic painting of a lighthouse. *Hokkaido University, Computing Centre, Japan*
134bl Simon Scofield when at Middlesex Polytechnic. *Courtesy of the artist*

Sculpture
135 William Latham, film still. *IBM UKSC Research Fellow*
137al William Latham, *Slugan 2. IBM UKSC Research Fellow*
137cr William Latham, *Mutation X. IBM UKSC Research Fellow*
137bl William Latham, *Tusk 9. IBM UKSC Research Fellow*
138 Rob Fisher, *Symphony of the Air*, Scotsdale, Arizona, computer-assisted environmental sculpture. *Photograph courtesy of the artist*
139 Rob Fisher, *Fandango*, Scotsdale, Arizona, computer-assisted environmental sculpture. *Photograph Courtesy the artist*
140 Kenneth Snelson, *Atomic Molecule*.
140–1 Kenneth Snelson, atoms at an exhibition. *Courtesy of the artist*

CHAPTER 4: TRANSFORMING REALITY

142–3 Jeffrey Shaw, detail of the *Legible City*, 1989–90. *Courtesy of the artist*

Interaction Design
145al Apple GUI. *Courtesy Apple Computer UK Ltd*
145cr Trimble Navgraphic. *Courtesy IDEO, USA*
145bl Apple GUI. *Courtesy Apple Computer UK Ltd*
146l Microsoft Windows 3. *Courtesy Microsoft Corporation*
146r HP New Wave. *Courtesy Hewlett Packard*
147l Sun Open Windows. *Courtesy Sun Microsystems*
147r DECwindows. *Courtesy Digital Corporation*
148 Virtuality 1000SD. *Courtesy W Industries, UK*
148–9b Cyberglove. *Courtesy Virtual Technologies*
149al Cyberglove. *Courtesy Virtual Technologies*

Virtual Reality
150 Architectural simulation by Gobbell Hays Partners Inc., winning first place in the Intergraph Graphic Users Group art competition, 1991. *Courtesy Intergraph Corporation*
151l Medical simulation, 'Breast Implant', by Bill Seneshen for Foresight Communications, using Alias software, 1991. *Courtesy Alias Research*
151c Fibre-optic helmet-mounted display by CAE Electronics Ltd. *Courtesy CAE Electronics Ltd*
152al Medical simulation, 'Architecture of the organ of Corti', © 1992 *Kyle A. McNeir, University of Illinois at Chicago, Department of Biomedical Visualization, SIGGRAPH*
152br Scientific visualization, 'The Five Non-Platonic Solids', © 1991 *John C. Hart and Thomas A. DeFanti, Electronic Visuals Lab., UIC, SIGGRAPH*
153 Alias Research, Scientific and Medical no. 1
154al Virtuality 1000 SU. *Courtesy W Industries, UK*
154br Virtuality 1000 SU. *Courtesy W Industries, UK*
155 BOOM, Fake Space Laboratories, Menlo Park, CA, 1991. *Courtesy Image Technology Branch: NASA Ames Research Centre*
156al BOOM, Fake Space Laboratories, Menlo Park, CA, 1991. *Courtesy Image Technology Branch: NASA Ames Research Centre*
156br Jeffrey Shaw, *Legible City*, 1989–90. *Courtesy of the artist*
156–7 Jeffrey Shaw, *Legible City*, 1989–90. *Courtesy of the artist*

Design for Process Data Visualization
160ar Pie chart. *Courtesy Polaroid Corporation*
160cl Pie chart and map. *Courtesy Polaroid Corporation*
161 Dennis Poon ATM. *Courtesy RCA, London*

Interactive Multimedia
163l Thatcher's cylindrical slide rule, 1881. *Courtesy Computer Museum, Boston, MA*
163r Sage AN/FSQ computer, 1958. *Courtesy Computer Museum, Boston, MA*
164 Hypercard screen. *Courtesy Design Museum, London*
165 Renaissance project, *Twelfth Night*, 1990. *Courtesy Art of Memory*
166 Garry Stewart, typographical tutorial, 1992. *Courtesy RCA, London*
167a Christian Batchelor, 'Ceroc: An interactive Dance Tutor', 1992. *Courtesy RCA, London*

167b Christian Batchelor, 'Architecture as Navigation', 1992. *Courtesy RCA, London*

168 Christian Batchelor, 'Architecture as Navigation', 1992. *Courtesy RCA, London*

Shape Grammar

171 R.A. and J.L. Kirsch, pseudo-Miró, 1990. *Courtesy of the Sturril Corporation, Clarksburg, MD*

172al Subjective comparison with Piet Mondrian's *Composition with Lines,* 1917. From *Studio International* special issue on 'Cybernetic Serendipity – The Computer and the Arts', Jasia Reichardt, London, 1968

172br Architectural design with shape grammar, student project, Hong Kong Polytechnic. *Courtesy William Fawcett*

173 Weissman Knight, *The Generation of Hepplewhite-style Chairback Designs*. Environment and Planning, University of California, Berkeley, CA, 1980. *Courtesy of the author*

Genetic Algorithms

176a William Latham, *Nine Mutations Branch Ribs*, 1991. *Courtesy IBM Scientific Centre, Winchester*

176b William Latham, *Nine Mutations*, 1991. *IBM UKSC Research Fellow*

177 William Latham, *Tree of Fractal Mutations*, 1991. *IBM UKSC Research Fellow*

178 William Latham, *Evolutionary Tree of Forms*, 1984. *Courtesy of the artist*

Rapid Prototyping

180–1 Stereolithography model for a car wheel. *Courtesy 3D Systems, Valencia, CA*

181l Lamination systems. *Courtesy of Norman Kinzie of Landform Technologies, Needham, MA, 1992*

181r Rapid prototyping. *Courtesy of Norman Kinzie of Landform Technologies, Needham, MA, 1992*

CHAPTER 5: TRANSFORMING TOMORROW

186–9 'Mapping the Information Business: Program on Information Resources Policy', John McLaughlin and Anne Louise Antonoff, Program on Information Policy Research, Harvard University, Cambridge, MA, 1986

190 Technology maps for the 1970s and 1980s. *Courtesy Apple Computer UK Ltd*

192 Earl Mark, 'Case Studies in Moviemaking and Computer-Aided Design', in *The Electronic Design Studio: Architectural Knowledge and Media in the Computer Era*, Malcolm McCullough, William Mitchell and Patrick Purcell, MIT Press, Cambridge, MA, 1990

193al Newton PDA. *Courtesy Apple Computer UK Ltd*

193br The EO palmtop notebook. *Courtesy EO Europe*

194c Music workstation, 1991. *Kenny Yip, RCA, London, Industrial Design*

194br Orbitor: interactive electronic globe system, 1991. *Shingo Kita, RCA, London, Industrial Design*

194–5a Aviator: interface for computer database, 1991. *Shingo Kita, RCA, London, Industrial Design*

195bl Terravellar: a traveller's guide. *Bettina Moellring, RCA, London, Industrial Design*

195r Electronic information finder. *Stefan Hillenmayer, RCA, London, Industrial Design*

INDEX

Figures in *italic* indicate pages on which illustrations appear. Figures in **bold** represent the main source of information on a particular topic.